PEGGY GUGGENHEIM COLLECTION

Father's Day 2010

Monica —
So sorry you aren't here
with us to celebrate the day.
Found this overview of
Peggy Guggenheim very
interesting. Hope you
enjoy it!
Love, Mosy

© 2005 Assouline Publishing
601 West 26th Street, 18th floor
New York, NY 10001, USA
Tel.: 212 989-6810   Fax: 212 647-0005
www.assouline.com

Color separation: Gravor (Switzerland)
Printed by Grafiche Milani (Italy)

ISBN: 2 84323 659 2

PEGGY GUGGENHEIM COLLECTION

PAOLO BAROZZI

ASSOULINE

i had met Peggy Guggenheim on various occasions in Venice, but our friendship really started the day I stopped to talk with her on the bridge in San Moisè, near Via XXII Marzo. It was a sunny day, and I was still wearing the air force uniform: my military service had come to an end, and in a few days I would be free again.

Peggy told me she was leaving for a journey to Greece and invited me to go with her; not thinking about it twice, I accepted. After being in the army for eighteen months, I had only one hope: to leave Venice and see the world. It was then that my journey in the world of contemporary art started, and Peggy became my guide. It was unusual for a Venetian like me—the heir of three generations of well-known antique dealers—to become interested in modern art. But I wanted to live in the present and forget about the glorious past of both Venice and my family. I shall never forget our departure from Venice: it was the first time I saw my city from the deck of a ship. I realized how important it was to see Venice from the sea in order to appreciate its incredible beauty. Intoxicated by the magical view, I imagined that the legendary woman at my side was an incarnation of the mythical Venice of the past, that *Serenissima,* "Queen of the Seas." The journey to Greece seemed to me the beginning of something new and exciting in my life, and I felt that maybe, with Peggy by my side, I would be able to make my dream come true and live a real life, escaping the destiny of a lazy existence among the lagoons. Peggy, influenced by the surrealists, told me that Venice was "the island of lotus eaters."

When we arrived in Athens, one of the first thing we did was to visit the Acropolis and the most important museums. I soon realized that what Peggy enjoyed most was to visit the Benachi Museum, which possesses one of the most important jewel collections in the world. She was buying antique earrings for her own collection, always searching for those made of gold, colored jewels, and mother-of-pearl, representing, in miniature, the ancient warships of the *Serenissima*'s fleet. I still have a photo of Peggy in which she is wearing two wonderful galleys. Our favorite pasttime was to discover the city, sit in open air cafés, and have delicious meals in charming little restaurants. In the evening, we often dined with Alan Ansen, the American poet (who also lived in Venice) at a big table with all of his friends, who were mostly writers and Beat poets.

during this journey, I had the opportunity to get to know Peggy better. She had been married to Max Ernst, who had left her for Dorothea Tanning; she had one son, Sindbad, and one daughter, Pegeen, from her first husband, Laurence Vail. I found the story she told me about the origins of her family very amusing and surreal: "I come from two of the best Jewish families. One of my grandfathers was born like Jesus Christ, in a stable—or rather, over a stable—in Bavaria, and my other grandfather was a peddler... If my grandfathers started life modestly, they ended it sumptuously. My stable-born grandfather, Mr. Seligman, came to America in the steerage, with $40 in his pocket, and contracted smallpox on board. He began his fortune by working as a roof shingler, and later by making uniforms for the Union Army in the Civil War. Some time after that, he became a renowned banker and the president of the

Temple Emanu-El. Socially, he got far beyond my other grandfather, Mr. Guggenheim, the peddler, who was born in Lengnau, in German Switzerland. Mr. Guggenheim far surpassed Mr. Seligman in amassing an enormous fortune and buying up most of the copper mines in the world, but he never succeeded in attaining Mr. Seligman's social distinction. In fact, when my mother married Benjamin Guggenheim, the Seligmans considered it a mésalliance. To explain that my mother was marrying into the well-known smelting family, they sent a cable to their kin in Europe saying, "Florette engaged Guggenheim smelter." This became a great family joke, as the cable was misread as "Guggenheim smelt her."

By the time I was born, the Seligmans and the Guggenheims were extremely rich. At least the Guggenheim were, and the Seligmans hadn't done so badly. My grandfather, James Seligman, was a very modest man who refused to spend money on himself and who under-fed his trained nurse. He lived sparsely and gave everything to his children and grandchildren. He remembered all our birthdays, and although he did not die until the age of 93, he never failed to make out a check on these occasions. The checks were innumerable, as he had eleven children and fifteen grandchildren.

Most of his children were peculiar, if not mad. One of my favorite aunts was an incurable soprano; if you happened to meet her on the corner of Fifth Avenue while waiting for a bus, she would open her mouth wide and sing scales, trying to make you do the same. She wore her hat hanging off the back of her head or tilted over one ear. A rose was always stuck in her hair. Long hatpins emerged dangerously, not from her hat but from her hair. Her trailing dresses swept the dust off the streets, and she invariably wore a feather boa. She also had a strange complex about germs, and was forever wiping her furniture with Lysol. But she had such extraordinary charms that I really loved her.

Another uncle lived on charcoal, which he had been eating for many years, and as a result his teeth were black. In a zinc-lined pocket he carried pieces of cracked ice, which he sucked all the time. He drank whiskey before breakfast and ate almost no food. He gambled heavily, as did most of my aunts and uncles, and when he was without funds he threatened to commit suicide to get more money out of my grandfather."

back in Venice, my friendship with Peggy flourished, and I visited her in her palace almost every day. By staying with her, I was learning a lot about modern art; she was a kind of university for me. Soon I began to be familiar with most of the works of art that were in her home.

The Peggy Guggenheim Collection is one of the world's foremost private collections of twentieth century art, and perhaps the only one in Europe to represent all of the most important movements that, from 1910 on, transformed the concept of art. This collection contains more than 200 works, among which, rare examples of the revolutionary spirit of twentieth century art: masterpieces from Dada and Russian Suprematism, works of the De Stijl group—in particular the two magnificent Mondrian drawings, dated 1912 and 1914, where one can perceive the future development of abstract art. Little by little, I learned to recognize every painting Peggy owned. I particularly liked the works of such surrealists as Ernst, Miró, Tanguy, Dalí, de Chirico, and Magritte, displayed in the *Barchessa* (a separate wing in Peggy's garden).

I was also fascinated by the large Picasso canvas *On the Beach*, at the entrance of the Palazzo. One day Peggy moved this large painting from the drawing room to the entrance, and at one point, while dragging this huge canvas of immense value, she unexpectedly stumbled, falling down flat on it. After the first moments of panic, we tried to check the damage she had caused to the painting. Falling on the Picasso, Peggy had left the imprint of her whole body. After inspecting the painting meticulously, she told me that a good restorer steeping it in the right places would succeed in making the cloth of the canvas as tight as it was before. Peggy also showed which parts of the painting had already been retouched.

Peggy always needed someone to help her during the days in which the collection was open to the public, and so I often did things for her. When I returned to Venice after working in the United States for almost two years, Peggy's daughter, Pegeen, convinced her mother to employ me to sell the paintings in the gallery of young artists she had created (situated in the basement, near the room with all the works by Jackson Pollock). Peggy did not like people to know that she was selling paintings in her home. In fact, she was mostly doing it to help Pegeen who had several children and always needed money. I also sold works by Peggy's other protégés, including Tancredi, Edmondo Bacci, Laurence Vail, and Bryon Gysin.

I took care of the gallery during the days when the museum was open to the public, and during the week I was Peggy's secretary. Those years back in the '60s were heroic: Peggy had to work very hard to keep the collection together, guarding and protecting her paintings.

In the morning, she would sleep rather late (if she did not have some important appointments), and after breakfast she made herself up and dressed. When she was ready, she went into the big living room, which had a fireplace, and there she spent her day working, seated at the large black desk always full of papers. Peggy seldom cooked, but when she was in the mood she was quite good at it: her specialty was shish kebab, her favorite dish.

In the afternoon, she often spent several hours listening to music (Vivaldi, Wagner, Mozart, Monteverdi), relaxing on one of the sofas lined with zebra skin, surrounded by her beloved dogs: Gypsy, Cillida, Sir Herbert, and Hong Kong.

People thought that Peggy was a rich American heiress, but it soon became clear that her reputation did not correspond to the truth. Even though she was not poor, Peggy lived beyond her means. She had a good income, but money was never enough. She had succeeded in assembling the best paintings of her collection by following a list established by her advisers, Herbert Reed and Marcel Duchamp. She had bought one masterpiece a day during the war in France, using all her ability to get low prices, as the Germans got nearer. Peggy was driven by an incredible force to vindicate her father and the many humiliations she had suffered as a young girl. She wanted to demonstrate to her uncles, the wealthiest patrons of the arts in the United States, that she, with little money, had been able to create an unique collection that, for the quality and rarity of the paintings, was far more important than those they had created with unlimited funds. Peggy adored her father; he had died in the *Titanic* disaster, and she wanted to rehabilitate his memory, as well as cancel her reputation as a bohemian with too many lovers.

I n the days preceding the First World War, the sinking of the *Titanic* was a tragedy without precedent, and Peggy, who was then 14, remained haunted by that nightmare. To find comfort, she became rather religious. She used to attend services in the Temple Emanu-El regularly taking great dramatic pleasure in standing up for the Kaddish (the service for the dead). It took her years to accept the death of her father. Maybe she never did, and for all her life she searched, in every man she fell in love with, for the father she had lost too soon.

When Peggy's father died, he left his affairs in an awful muddle. Not only had he lost a vast fortune by discontinuing his partnership with his brothers, but the money he should have had (some $8,000,000) he had also lost in Paris. The small amount that was left was tied up in stocks that yielded no interest and were at such a low ebb that they could not be sold. Peggy's mother did not know this, and the family continued to live on the same grandiose scale. Peggy's uncles, the Guggenheims, advanced all the money that Peggy and her mother needed, keeping them in supreme ignorance. Finally, her mother discovered the truth and took drastic steps to end the false situation; she started spending her own personal fortune and moved to a cheaper apartment with fewer servants. She also sold her paintings, her tapestries, and her jewelry. She managed very well, but although they were never poor, from that moment on Peggy developed a complex about no longer being a real Guggenheim. She felt like a poor relative and suffered great humiliation thinking how inferior she was, compared to the rest of the family. Soon, she developed a strong need to be successful in life, to be "someone," whatever the cost.

Peggy realized that if her father had remained an active member of his brothers' business society, Mr. Guggenheim & Sons, her mother would have inherited something like $800,000,000 and she would have been very rich. Peggy's father, Benjamin Guggenheim, had paid a high price for freedom, leaving his brothers before they earned an immense fortune from the copper mines of Chuquicamata, in Chile. In Venice, I realized that Peggy had never resigned herself to loosing her father's inheritance, which she thought was hers by right. Even though she largely regained her lost inheritance thanks to her paint-ings, I remember that when the experts of the insurance companies came to Venice to evaluate the paintings, Peggy was astonished to see the huge amounts at which they were insured. Smiling, she would say: "Now they are worth millions, but I paid almost nothing for them!"

Peggy was born in New York City, on West 69th Street, in 1898. Her mother had told her that while the nurse filled her hot water bottle, she rushed into the world with her usual speed and screamed like a cat. She had two sisters, Hazel and Benita; Benita was her favorite. Peggy once said to me: "My childhood was excessively unhappy; I have no pleasant memories of any kind."

Peggy had no early interest in modern art. In fact, she first loved and studied Italian Renaissance painting, particularly that of Venice. Nevertheless, in 1938 she had the idea of opening a modern museum in London. With her usual flair for enlisting the ablest guidance, she asked Herbert Read to become the director of the projected museum. The collection was begun and a building was found, but the Second World War erupted, and she could only keep her gallery, Guggenheim Jeune, open for a few month. In Paris, Peggy courageously kept adding to the collection, "buying a picture a day." She even rented space for a gallery on place Vendôme, but the cool war turned hot. Brancusi's *Bird in Space* was bought as the Germans were nearing Paris. In the spring of 1941, the collection and its owner reached New York, and later, in 1942, Peggy opened her famous gallery, Art of This Century.

I n Venice, while waiting for customers to buy works by young artists, I started a diary about all the interesting things that were going on at the palace. I also became a journalist for *Il Mondo*, a magazine directed by Mario Pannunzio. One of the first interviews I did was with Peggy, regarding her relationship with

Jackson Pollock. On that occasion, she told me, "He was very tall, with broad shoulders, and his eyes were like those of a ferret. I think he was rather bald. He was shy and rather sweet, and when he was not drunk he was remote and difficult to communicate with. It seemed that everything was going on only inside himself, and no one was allowed access. He was like a trapped animal that never should have left Wyoming, where he was born."

When Peggy met Jackson Pollock for the first time, the artist was seriously broke. In January of 1943, Pollock was making ends meet by working as a part-time custodian at the Museum of Non-Objective Painting, also known as the Solomon R. Guggenheim Collection. In other words, at the time Peggy discovered him, Pollock was working for her uncle!

Luckily for Pollock, Peggy was about to divorce Max Ernst and was eagerly looking for a new group of artists to promote in her gallery. Roberto Matta and Howard Putzel introduced her to Pollock in 1943. Pollock showed his first painting at Peggy's new gallery Art of This Century, located at 30 West 57th Street, for the Spring Salon for Young Artists (May 18-June 26, 1943). His painting, *Stenographic Figure*, received a strong positive response, including a glowing mention in the magazine, *The Nation*. The result, as Pollock reported to his brother Charles in July of 1943, was: "I have a year's contract with the Art of This Century, and a large painting to do for Peggy Guggenheim's house…with no strings as to what I paint." The work Pollock subsequently created for Peggy's new house would be his breakthrough large painting, *Mural*. Presenting Pollock's first show to the press, Peggy said it was "an event in the contemporary history of American art." The review in *The New York Times* agreed, raving, "Pollock's talent is volcanic!"

In subsequent months, more critical opinions would emerge strongly in Pollock's favor. "Pollock is in a class by himself," the influential critic Clement Greenberg would observe. Years later, in 1952, Greenberg added, "Others may have greater gifts or maintain a more even level of success, but no painter in this period realizes so strongly, so truly, or so completely. Pollock does not offer samples of miraculous handwriting, he gives us achieved and perfected works of art."

Pollock's first large work, *Mural,* was painted on canvas at the suggestion of the surrealist painter Marcel Duchamp. That way, the work could be moved, shown, and sold—unlike ordinary murals painted directly onto plaster.

Like Peggy—though for very different reasons—Pollock soon began moving away from the surrealists: he had become disillusioned with Jungian analysis, and mythic symbolism no longer appealed to him. Instead he began to concentrate on abstract patterns and rhythms and to experiment with new painting techniques, which included working from a raw canvas lying on the floor. "I feel nearer, more a part of the painting," he would explain, "since this way I can walk around it, work from the four sides and literally be in the painting. This is akin to the method of the Indian painters of the West."

between 1943 and 1947, Pollock had three solo shows at Art of This Century. The gallery created for Peggy by the avant-garde architect Friedrich Kiesler was very spectacular, and people were queued up to visit it. The press gave the new gallery a huge amount of publicity. No one had seen anything like it before: it was a big space with many rooms in which various exhibits took place at the same time. Art of This Century soon became a most vital center of avant-garde American art, and Peggy Guggenheim was the first to exhibit the great new American painters—Jackson Pollock, Robert Motherwell, William Baziotes, Clifford Still, and Mark Rothko—thus influencing the development of American art after the war. From that moment, Peggy could say that she had won. She had become what she had always wanted to be: "a living legend." To continue would have been folly, and she decided it was the right time to retire. She wanted to leave New York, the city where she was born, and go back to Europe—to settle in her favorite city with her collection.

Peggy had always loved Venice. She had visited, many times, but it was only in 1948, when she was invited to exhibit her collection at the XXIV Biennale (in the Greek Pavilion, which was available because the country was at war), that she decided to stay. She loved the city and lived in an imaginary Venice created by her favorite writers, like Henry James—this might have been the reason she was so often disappointed with Venetians of the day. One of her greatest pleasures was to go out in her gondola, or to walk around Venice followed by her many dogs (all of them belonged to a rare breed: Lhasa Apso, originally from Tibet, the Dalai Lama's sacred dogs).

In the summer of 1960, I had the opportunity to act in a masque written for Peggy's birthday and for the arrival, in Venice, of the poet James Merrill. The show featured Alan Ansen, John Myers, Niki and Frank Amey, and Meg Munday. But the real show was what went on behind the scenes during rehearsals: we had to wait for those who were late, and then the beatniks started to drink and ended up making dramatic scenes for no reason and deciding to change all the furniture in the room in order to create the right atmosphere.

I was fascinated by the incredible conversations that went on between Alan Ansen and Gregory Corso. Ansen, a friend of Bowels, Burroughs, Ginsberg, and Kerouac, was the most eccentric person in Venice. He was tall as a giant and used to dress up in the most extraordinary outfits. I still remember how much I laughed the day the

American fleet arrived in Venice, when I saw him in campo San Stefano with a bottle of whiskey in one hand, dressed up in flaming red, running toward the dock like a crazy bull.

Our masque attracted all the important foreign eccentrics in Venice—of which Peggy was the undisputed queen. Everyone wore tuxedos, with black masks on their faces and a cockade made of multicolored ribbons on their lapels.

The Beats also told me a funny story about Marlon Brando. A few years before, the star had come to Venice for the film festival (to receive a prize for his performance in *A Streetcar Named Desire*); one evening when he was bored, Brando was told that Peggy was giving a big party at her palace, and decided to go. But he entered Peggy's house wearing blue jeans and a T-shirt, and Peggy, not knowing who he was, had him thrown out by her servants. She regretted it bitterly the next morning when she read about it in the newspapers.

After I met Mr. Stanley Marcus at an exhibition in Venice, he offered me a chance to work for him, for at least six months, in Dallas. So I accompanied Peggy, in her gondola, to a happening organized by Jean-Jacques Lebel—it was called "The Funérailles de la Chose de Tinguelly" and took place on the Giudecca Canal—and then I left for America.

after Dallas, I went to New York and worked there during one of the most stimulating periods of American history: the Kennedy era. It coincided with a major artistic revolution. I often visited the Leo Castelli Gallery, then a focal point of what was taking place in the world of American paintings. Through Ivan Karp, Leo Castelli's secretary, I got in touch with new artists who were starting to become well-known.

I saw Roy Lichtenstein's first paintings, and following Karp's introduction, I visited Andy Warhol at his first factory. I went to James Rosenquist's immense loft on Broadway and visited Claes Oldenburg in the Lower East Side studio where he was showing his "store," displaying and selling his sculptures of such things as pies and pantyhose, as though in a department store.

I was enthusiastic about the works of those young New York artists and arranged with them an exhibition of their works in Italy. Back in Venice, I was eager to share my discovery with Peggy, and one day I asked her if she was willing to do that show with me. Peggy's reaction, however, was like a cold shower: she did not like pop art and thought it was a degenerate art done by advertising designers.

During the winter, Peggy's collection was closed, and I often went back to New York; there, I quickly realized that if after the war the most important painter had been Jackson Pollock, his place had now been taken by Andy Warhol, "the prince of nothing, the sphinx without secrets." Warhol often came to Venice for the Biennale vernissage and I sometimes saw him at the film festival, promoting his underground movies. At the time, Warhol was mainly interested in doing portraits of famous people. He had actually asked me to find rich customers who would commission a portrait for $25,000. Warhol also asked me to introduce him to Peggy in order to do her portrait, but she always refused to have him in her house.

Peggy was a passionate reader, and she befriended famous writers. In the silence of Venice, she had perhaps regretted not being a great writer. During the winter, she would nevertheless dedicate many hours to the writing of her memoirs. Since her stay in Paris, back in the '20s, with Laurence Vail, Peggy had always sought the company of writers. She had met James Joyce, had been in love with Samuel Beckett, and was a close friend of the poetess Djuna Barnes (whom she helped financially for many years). Mary McCarthy was with her in Venice when she decided to buy Palazzo Venier dei Leoni, and Truman Capote was her guest in the Venetian palace when he wrote a part of *The Muses are Heard*.

What did Peggy do for Venice? In 1948, she organized a sculpture exhibition in her garden; it included *L'angelo della cittadella*, by Marino Marini, which Peggy had bought in Milan from the artist. The sculpture gave rise to a scandal owing to the realism of its anatomic details. In 1950, Peggy was proud to personally organize, for the Museo Correr, a retrospective on Jackson Pollock.

In 1954 she met Max Ernst again. He was in Venice to receive the Biennale Grand Prize, and Peggy had the opportunity to make peace with him after years of mutual misunderstandings.

In 1962 Peggy was made honorary citizen of Venice, and that same year she exhibited her collection at the Tate Gallery in London. I was with her for the opening, and during my stay in London I had the opportunity to meet Francis Bacon. Peggy told me a funny story about him: "One night the king of London's thieves tried to break into Bacon's house. He was walking carefully on the roof when he lost his balance, smashed the skylight of the painter's studio, and ended up falling in Bacon's bed. This incident was decisive for both men: from that moment on, they never separated."

In 1966, there was a terrible flood in Venice and the city was completely under water for twenty-four hours. Peggy was seriously concerned by the dramatic problem of the city's future and gave her financial help to this cause.

In the spring of 1966, Peggy telephoned me early one morning and said, "Marcel Duchamp and Teenie are in Venice. You can come with us. Please reserve a table at the restaurant Malamocco." Peggy and Duchamp were great friends, and she had told me a lot of things about him. I was very curious to meet Duchamp, having admired *Sad Young Man in a Train* in Peggy's collection. I enjoyed Duchamp's humor; everything seemed to be a game, and although he was famous, he did not take himself seriously. Speaking to him over lunch, I realized that this man's most important achievement was himself, "a living work of art."

Peggy had always been of the opinion that the collection should stay in Venice forever, and she used all her diplomatic skills to make it possible. She tried to donate her collection to some of the most important museums in the world, but without success. She knew that she did not have enough money to keep the collection in Venice, and if she left it to her children, they would sell the paintings when in need of money, and ruin the work of her life. In the end, she decided to forget her old grudges against her uncle Solomon and left her collection to the Guggenheim Museum in New York. In 1969 the Guggenheim in New York invited her to exhibit her collection. It was during her stay in New York that she reached an accord with her cousin Harry regarding the future of the collection: "The collection would remain in Venice, intact, in her name, to be administered by them, and nothing was to be removed."

When Peggy died, in 1979, the Palazzo Venier dei Leoni and the collection had become the propriety of the Solomon R. Foundation. The palace has since been completely restored, and the collection is open to the public six days a week for seven months a year.

Peggy created a collection that was unique in the world, and she succeeded in making certain that it would always remain in Venice. Thus, her favorite city symbol of the past would remain linked to the present, thanks to the masterpieces of her collection.

I often enjoyed reading what Peggy wrote about Venice: "Every hour of the day is a miracle of light. In summer, with daybreak, the rising sun produces such a tender magic on the water that it nearly breaks one's heart. As the hours progress, the light becomes more and more violet, until it envelops the city with a diamond-like haze. Then it commences slowly to sink into the magic sunset, the *capolavoro* of the day. This is the moment to be on the water. It is imperative. The canals lure you, call you, cry to you to come and embrace them from a gondola. More pity to those who cannot afford this poetic luxury. In this brief hour, all of Venice's intoxicating charm is poured forth on its waters. It is an experience never to be forgotten. Day after day, one is drawn from terra firma to float in the lagoon, to watch the sunset, or to go gently past the palaces, seeing their images reflected in the canal. The reflections are like paintings more beautiful than any painted by the greatest masters. The striped *Pali,* when seen in the water, deny their functional use and appear like colored snakes. If anything can rival Venice in its beauty, it must be its reflection at sunset in the Grand Canal…" (From *Invitation to Venice* by Michelangelo Muraro, with photographs by Ugo Mulas, Edizioni Mursia 1962.)

One of the last times I saw Peggy, I asked her to tell me what was the meaning of art for her. Answering at once, without hesitation—maybe remembering the famous verse from Shakespeare's *The Tempest*—she said, "Such stuff as dreams are made on…"

In my bedroom in Venice, hanging near my bed, there is a dream catcher; it is an aquamarine circle made of leather, embellished with pearls, and multicolored feathers. It is an amulet that Peggy gave me as a present one day she was coming back from New York. Some nights, when the wind is blowing on the lagoons, my dream catcher starts to whirl, and looking at it, I like to think that Peggy's heritage has been to teach me how to dream in a world in which nobody seemed to dream anymore.

Among my favorite souvenirs, there is an old postcard that Peggy sent me from a trip in the East. With time it has become yellowish; it represents an old mosque with a few wonderful golden domes and a minaret. Peggy wrote on it, "On the tracks of Tamerlane going to Samarcanda."

Every time I read that postcard, I feel like I am getting ready to leave for an exciting new journey, on the verge of a fantastic adventure, with Peggy at my side.

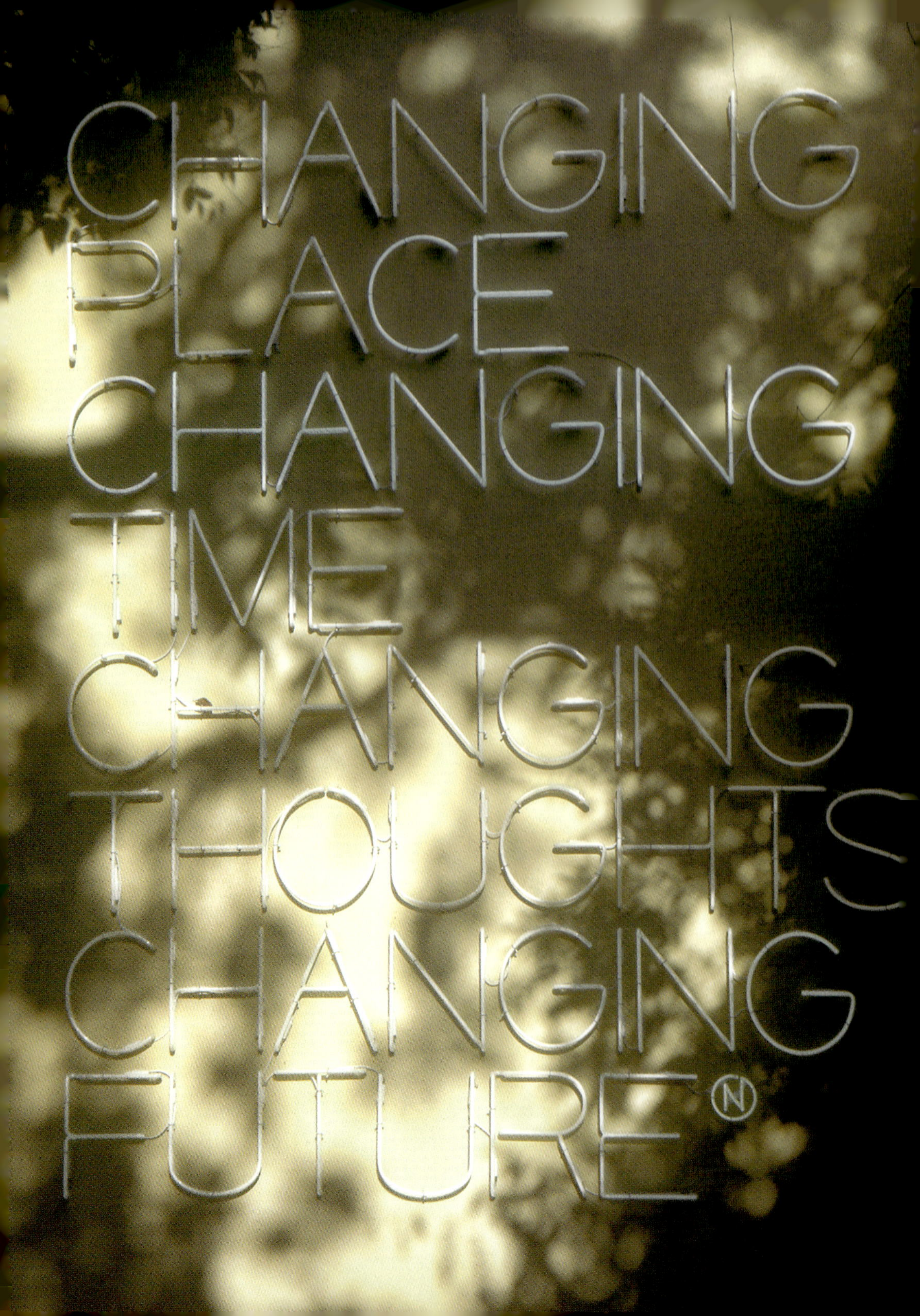

CHANGING
PLACE
CHANGING
TIME
CHANGING
THOUGHTS
CHANGING
FUTURE

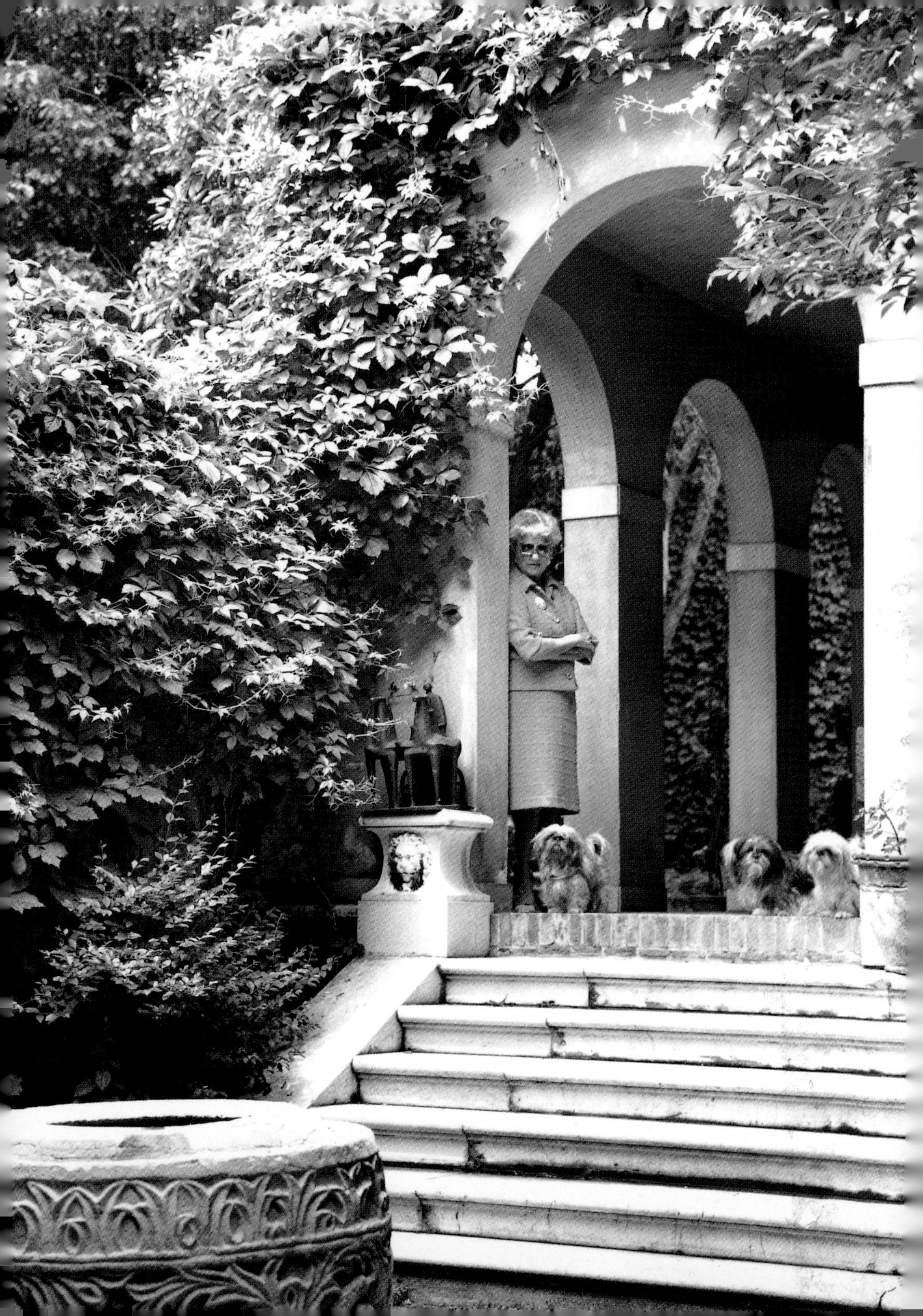

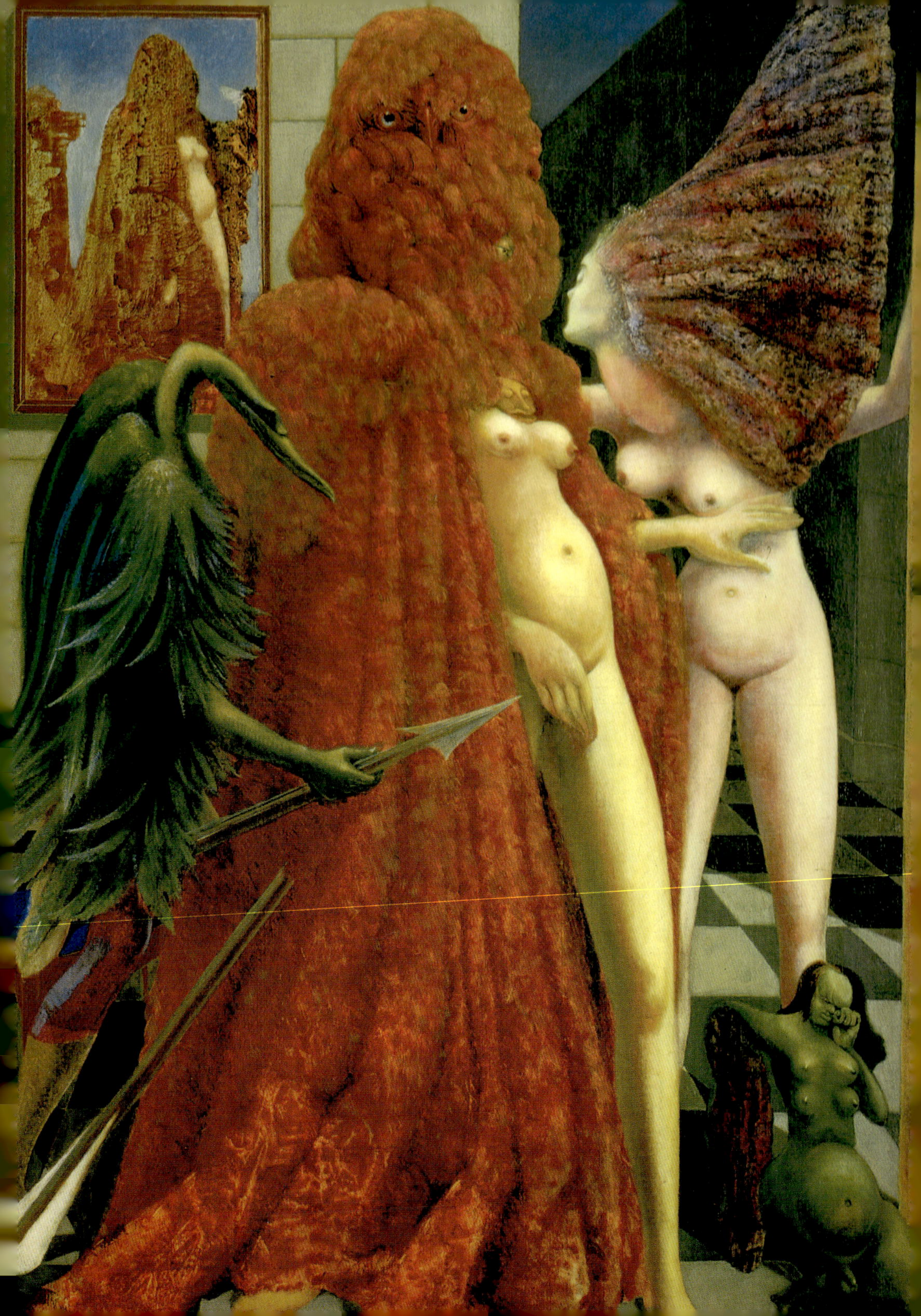

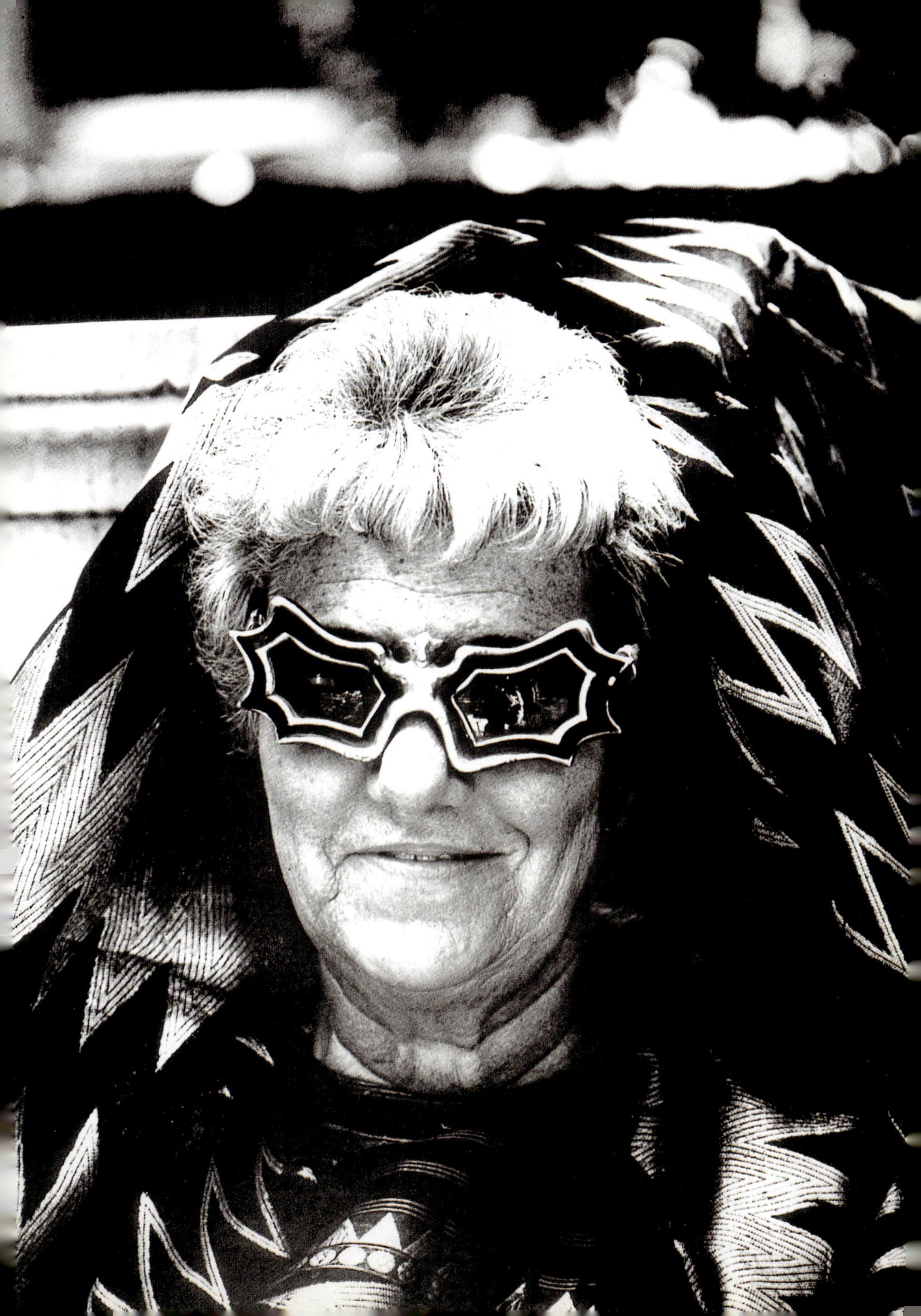

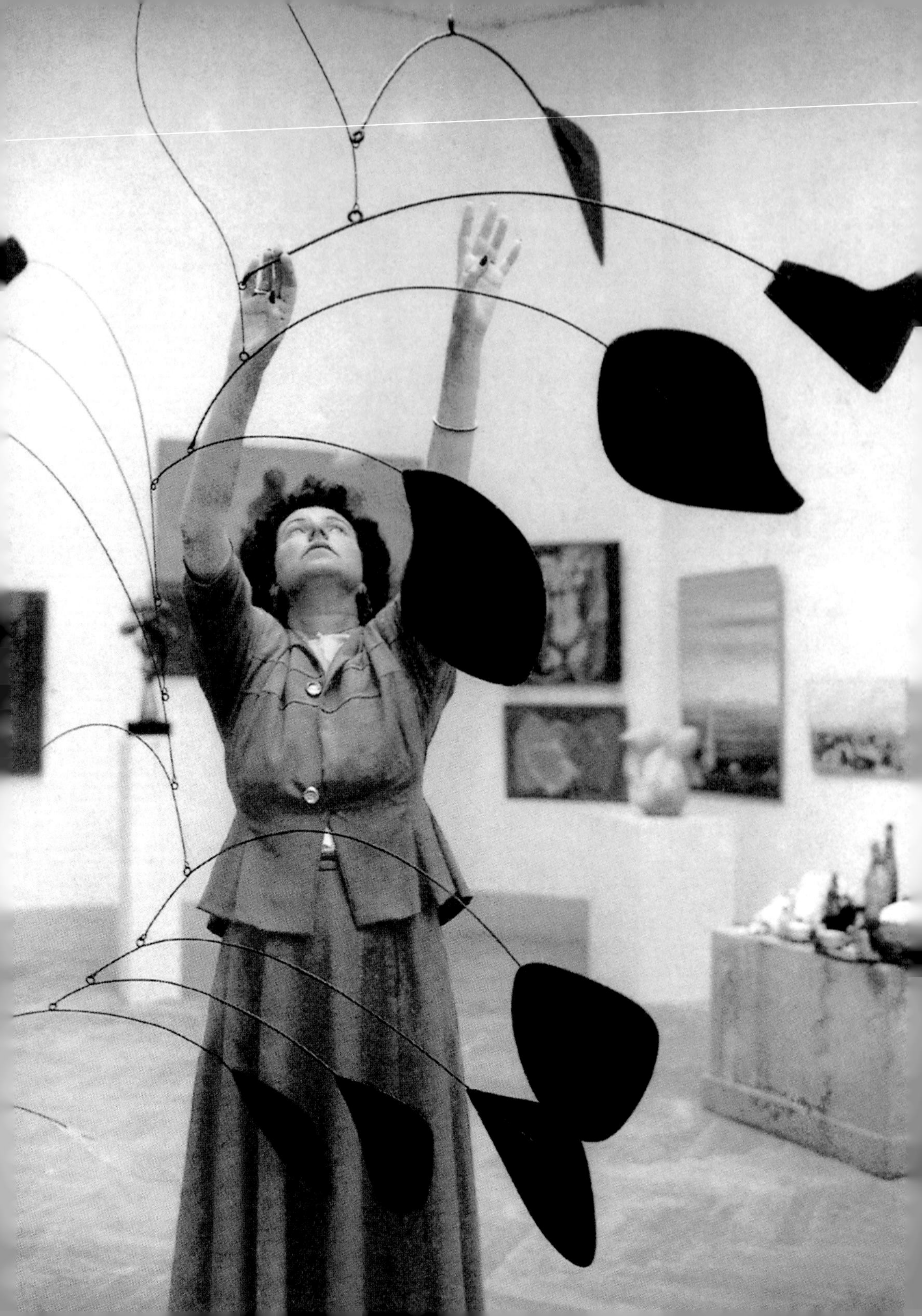

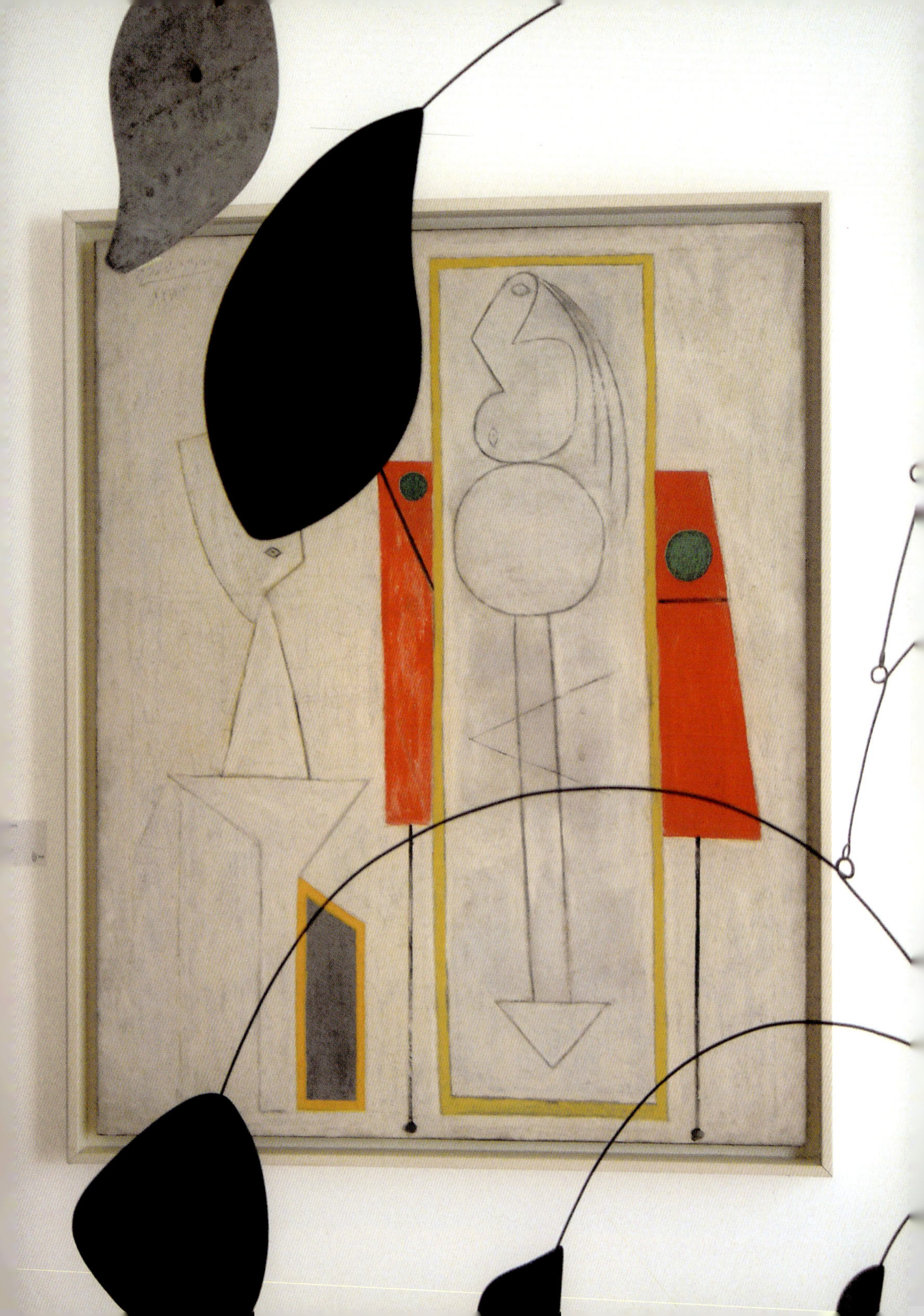

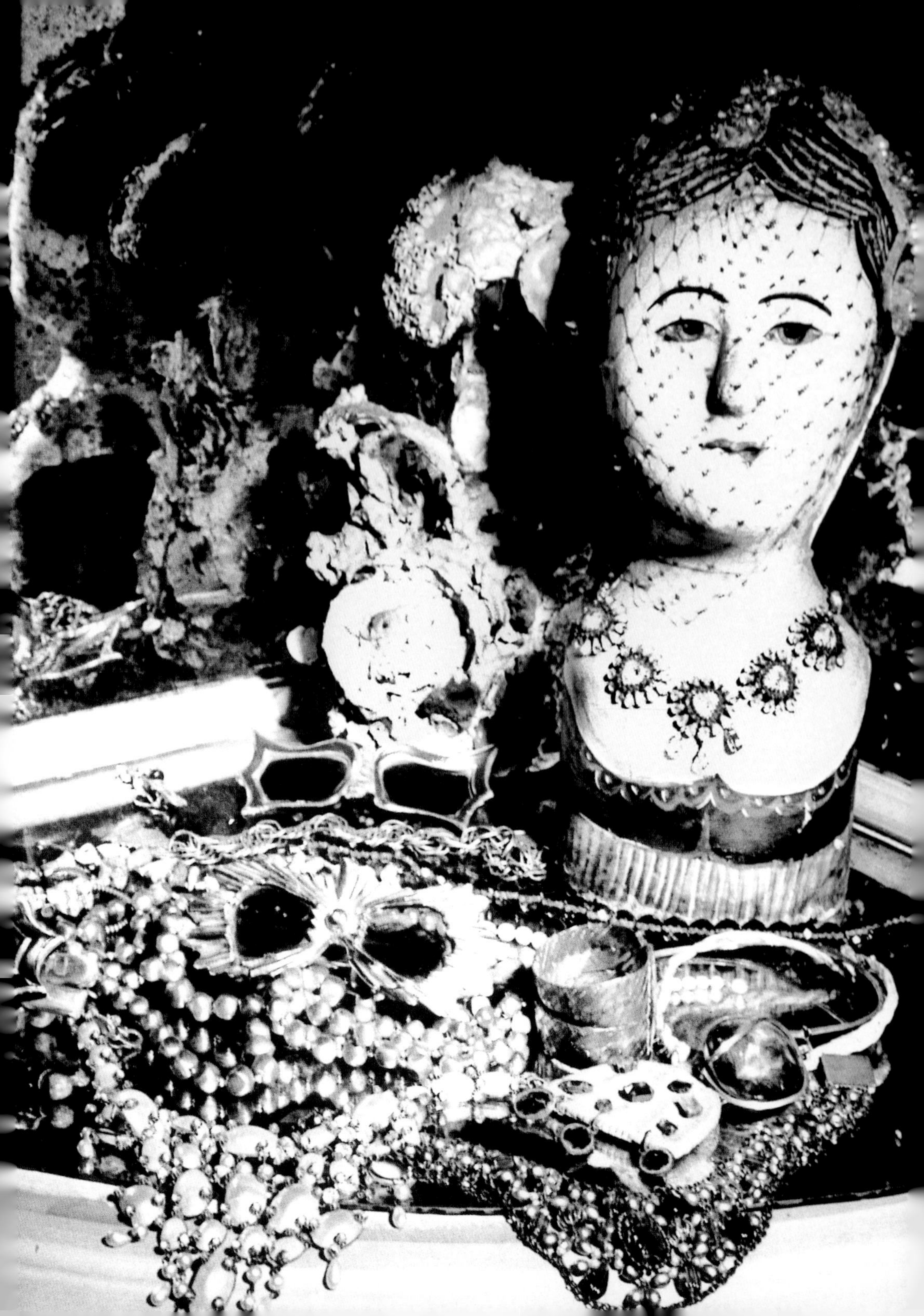

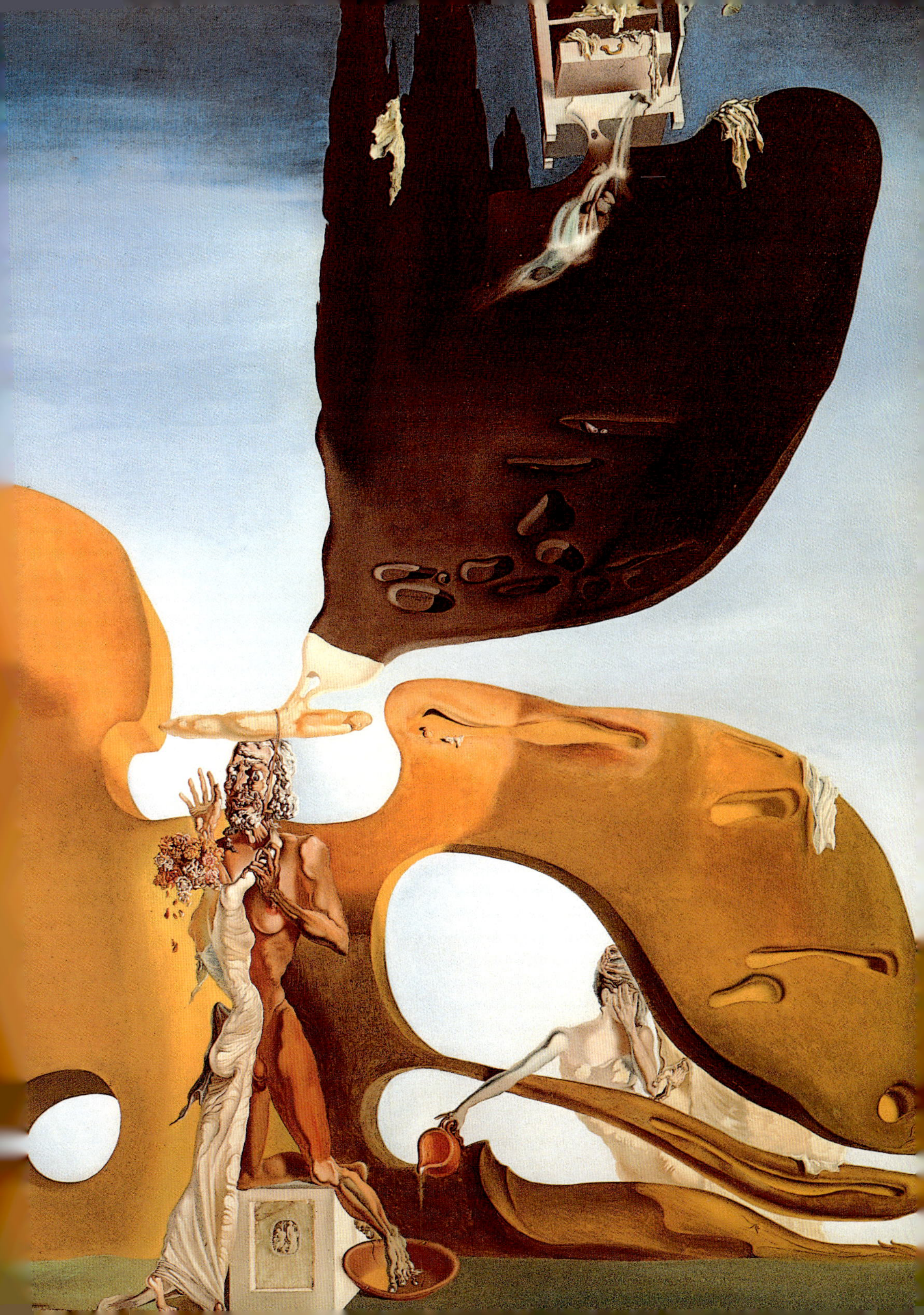

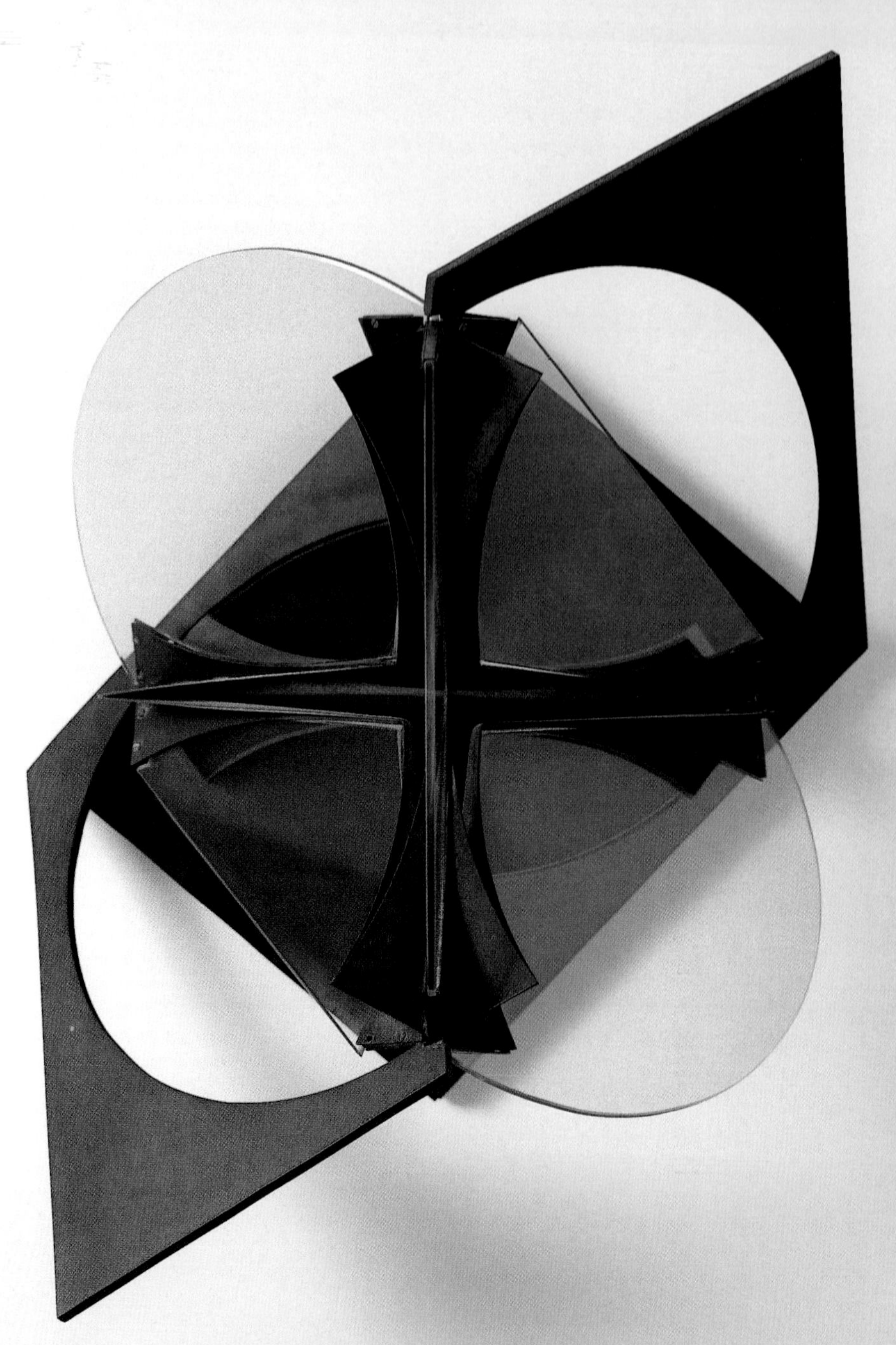

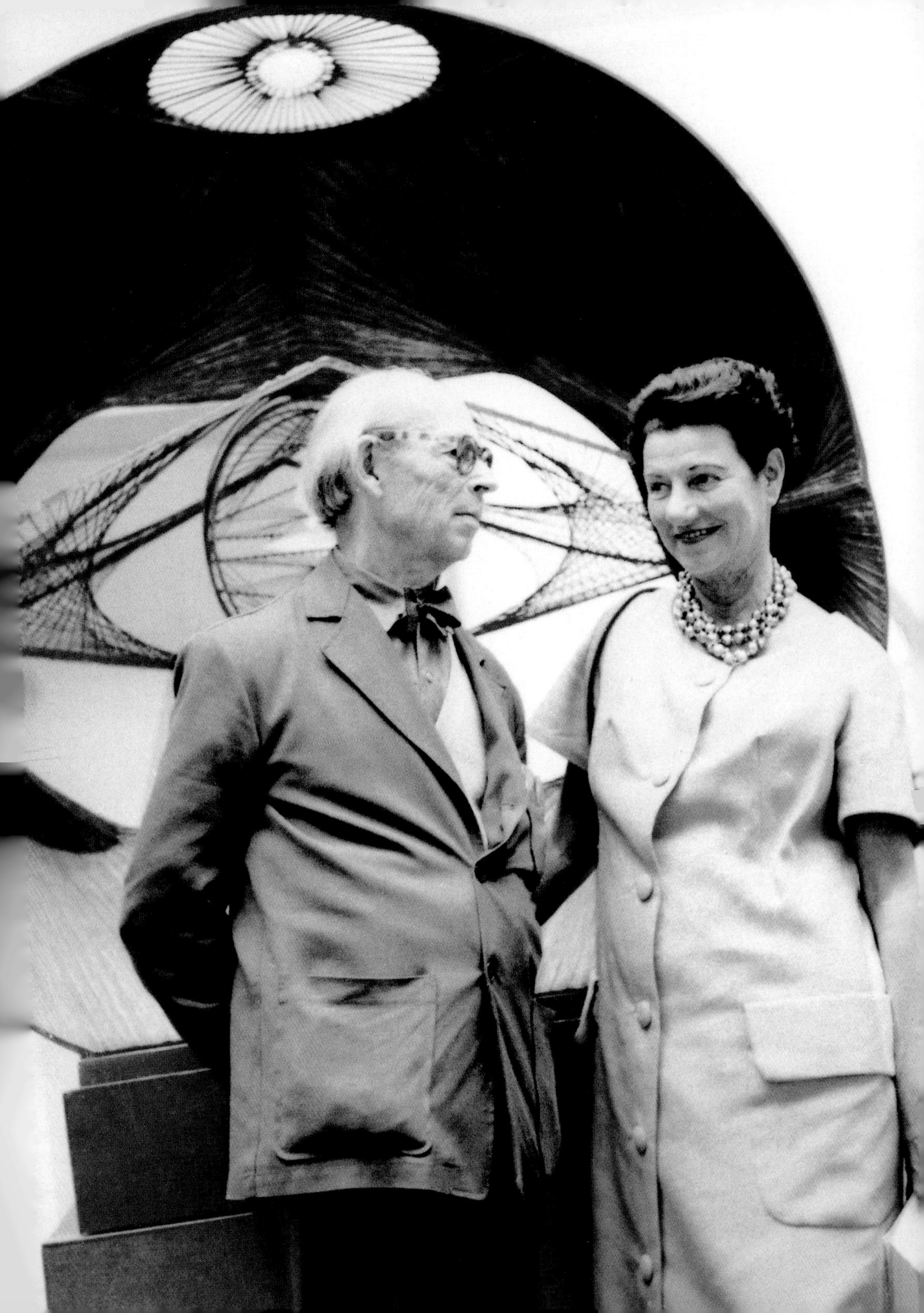

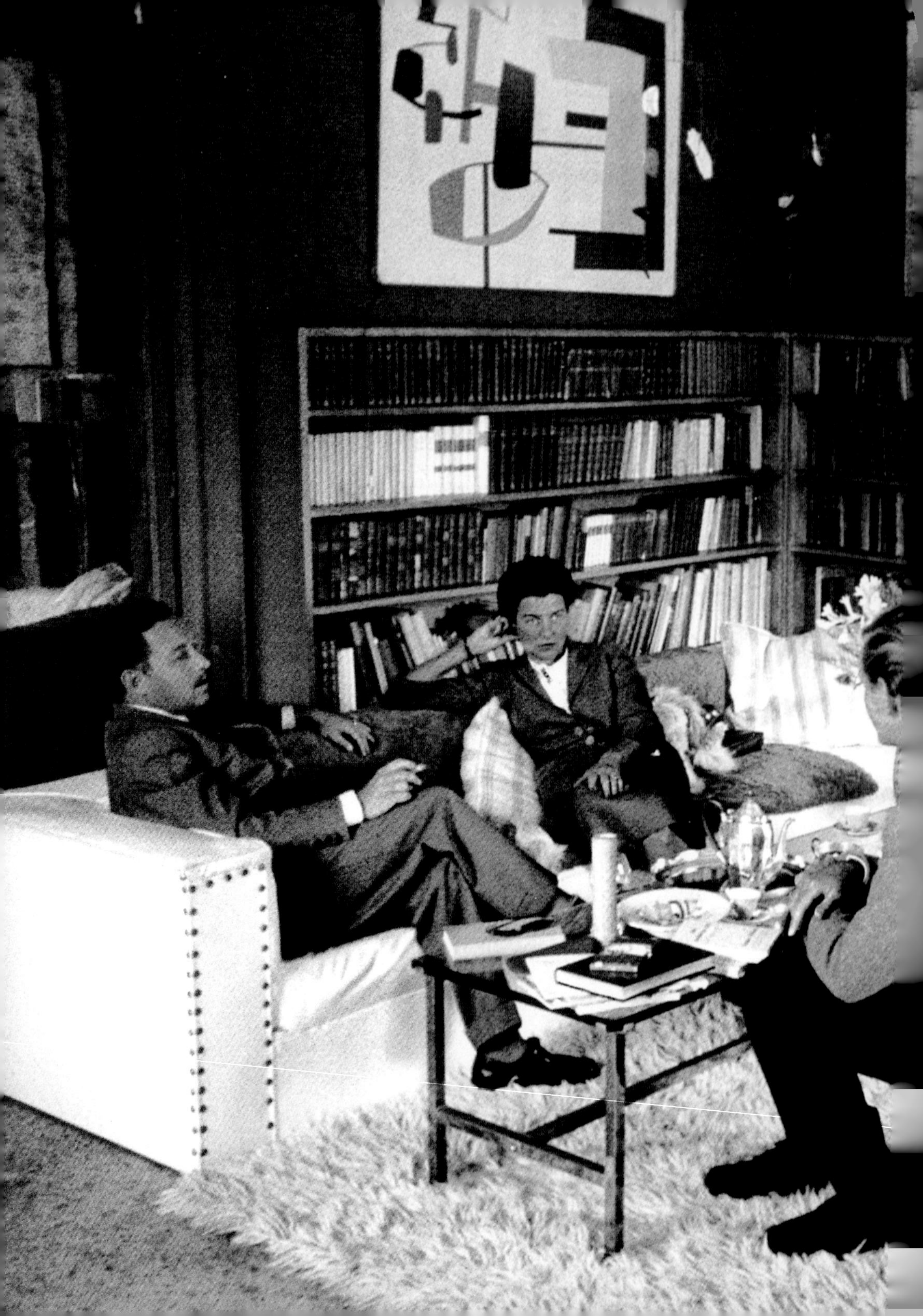

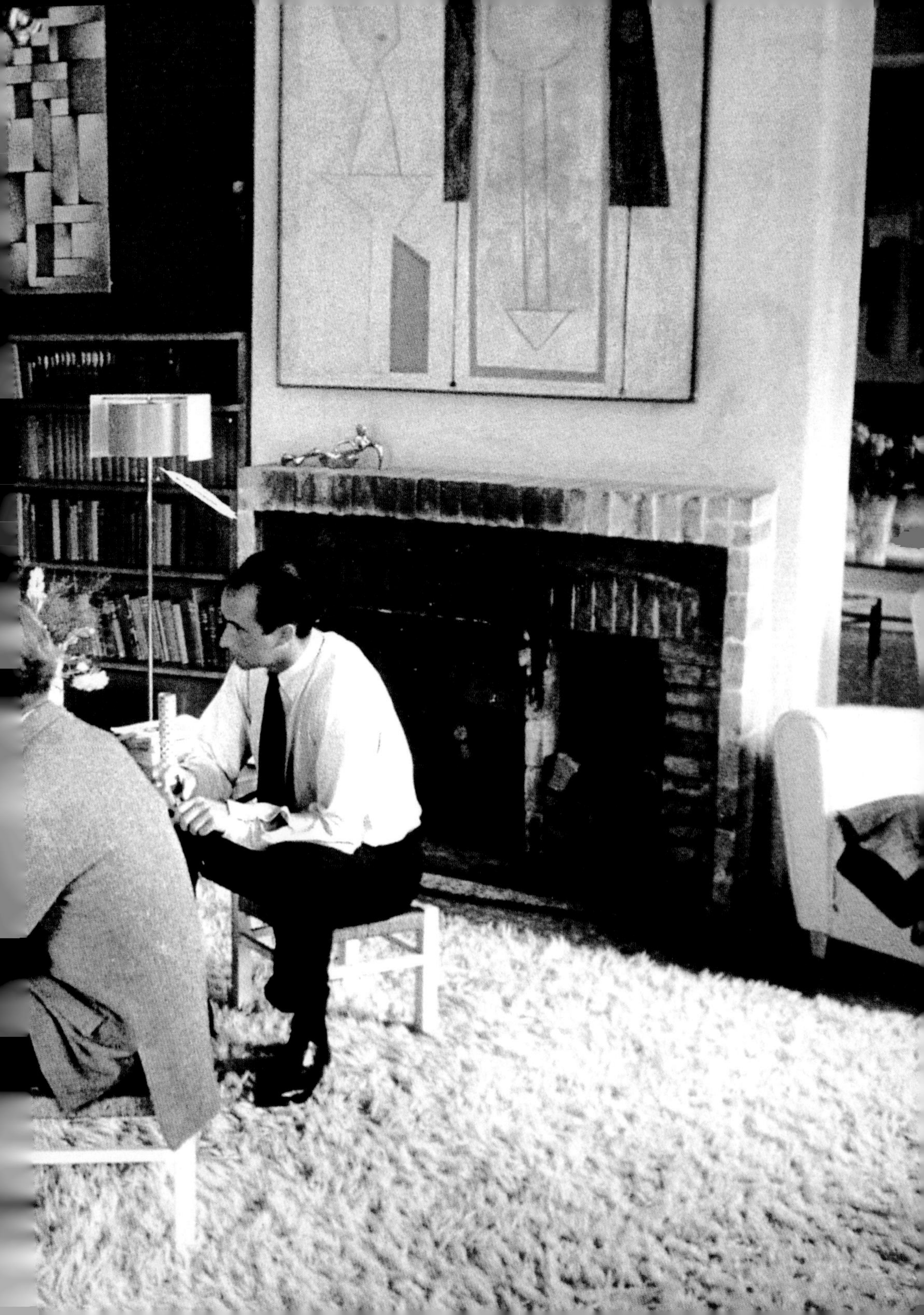

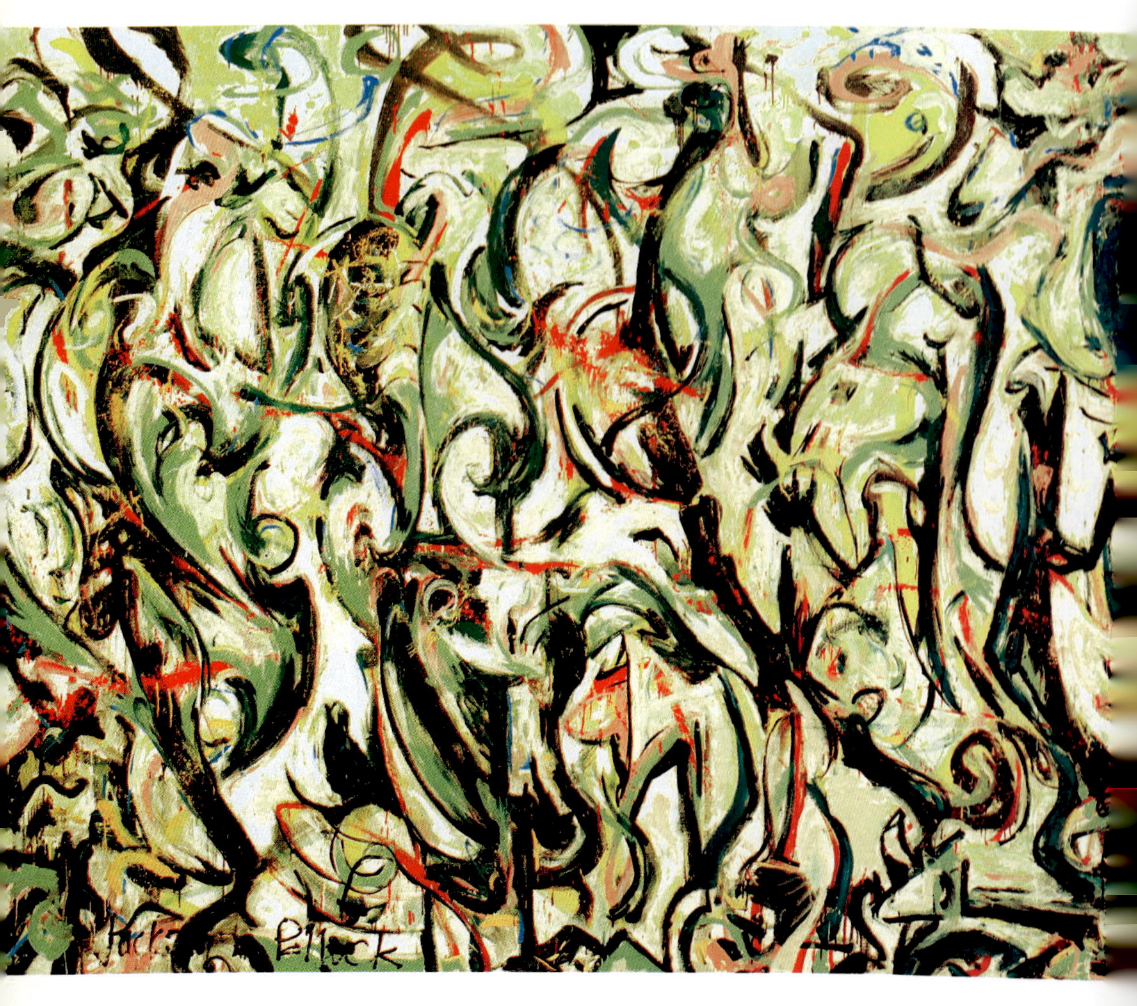

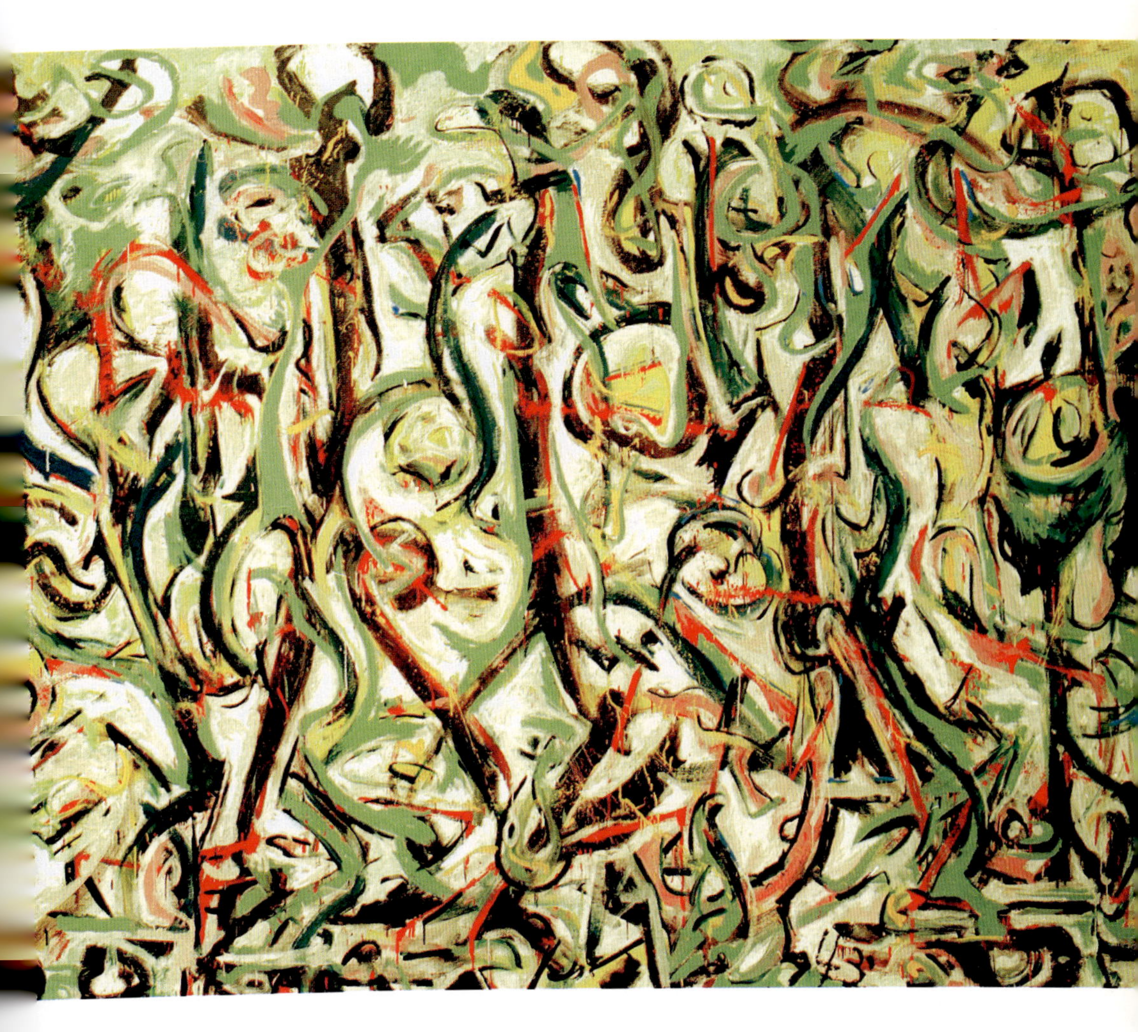

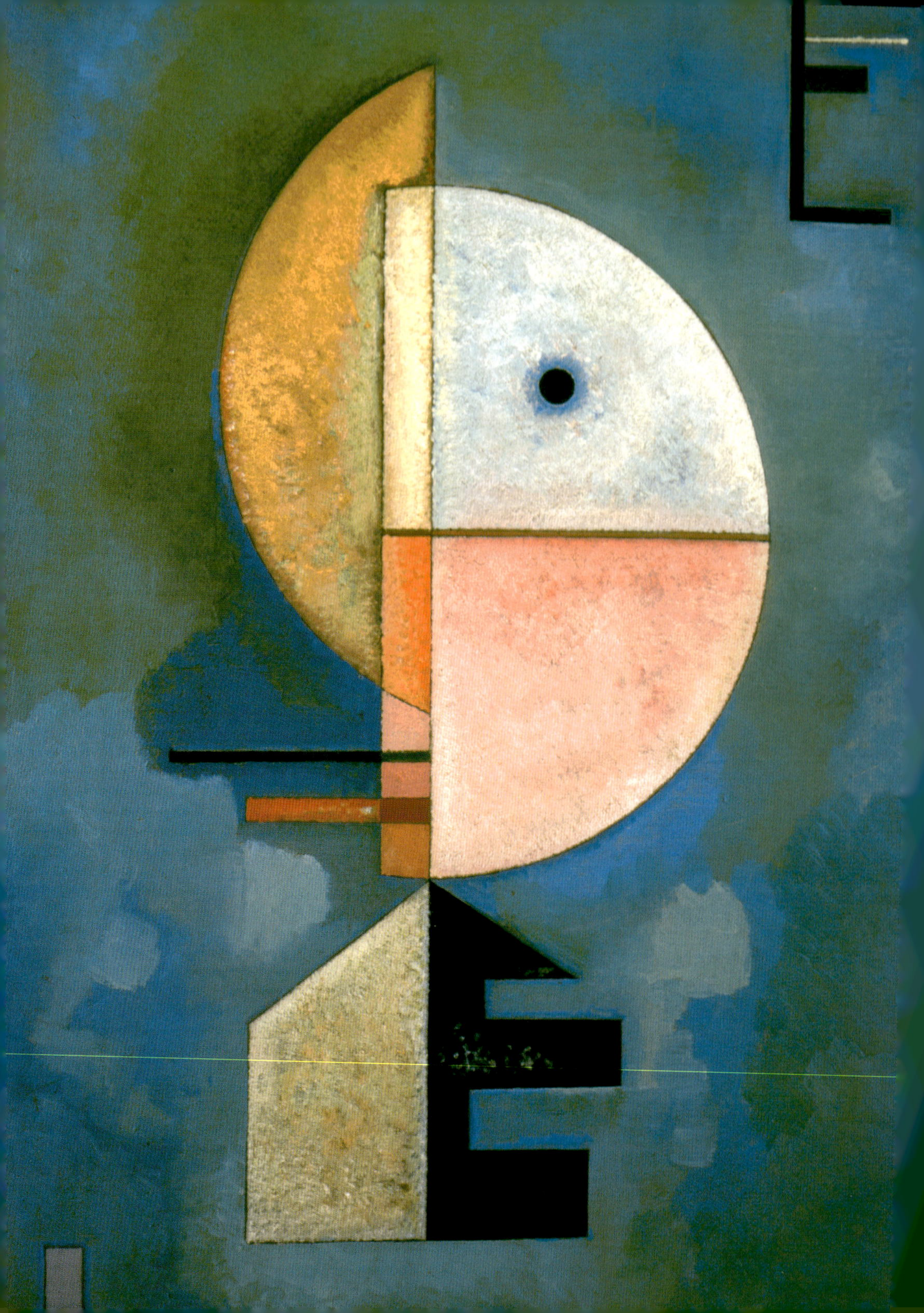

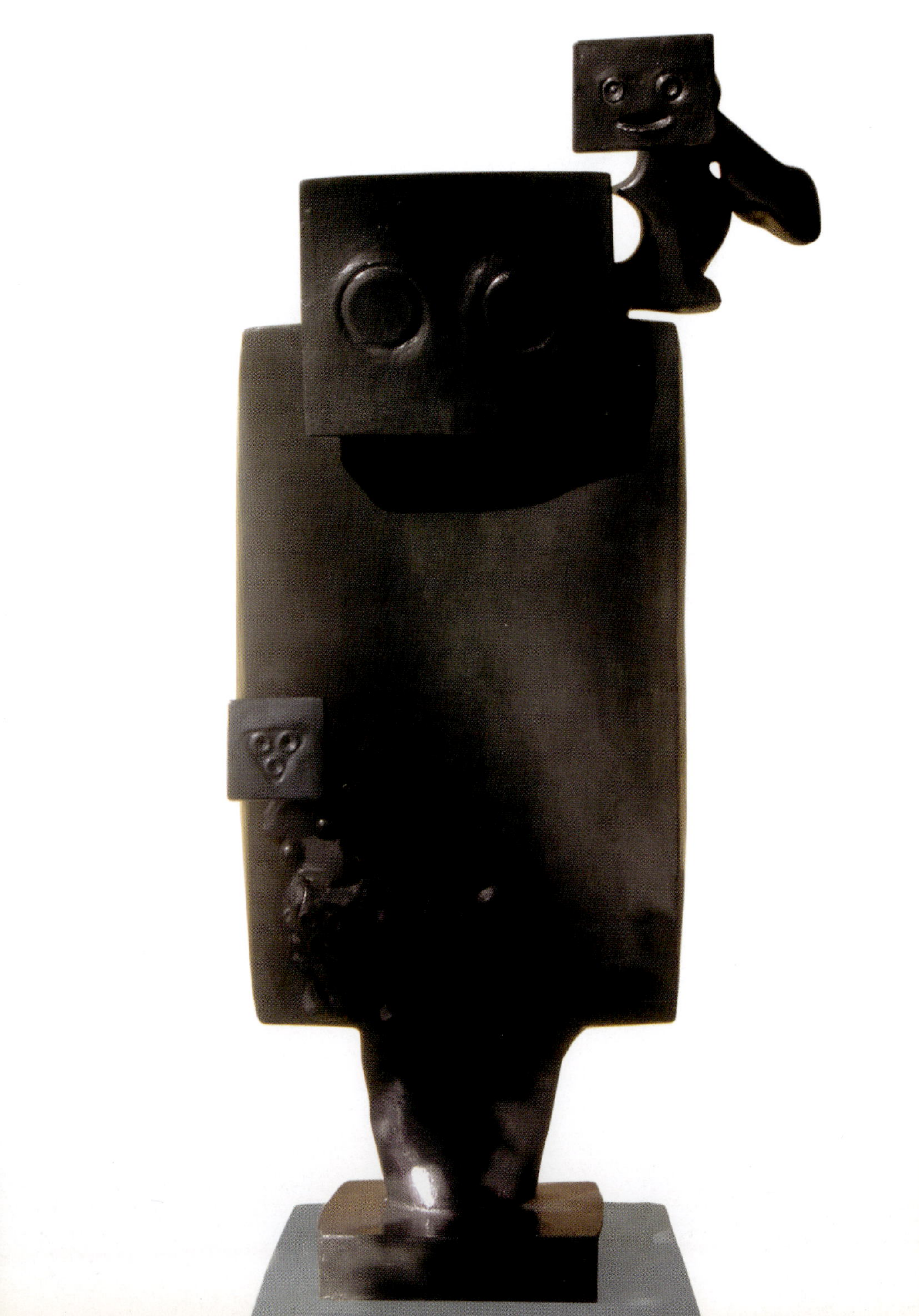

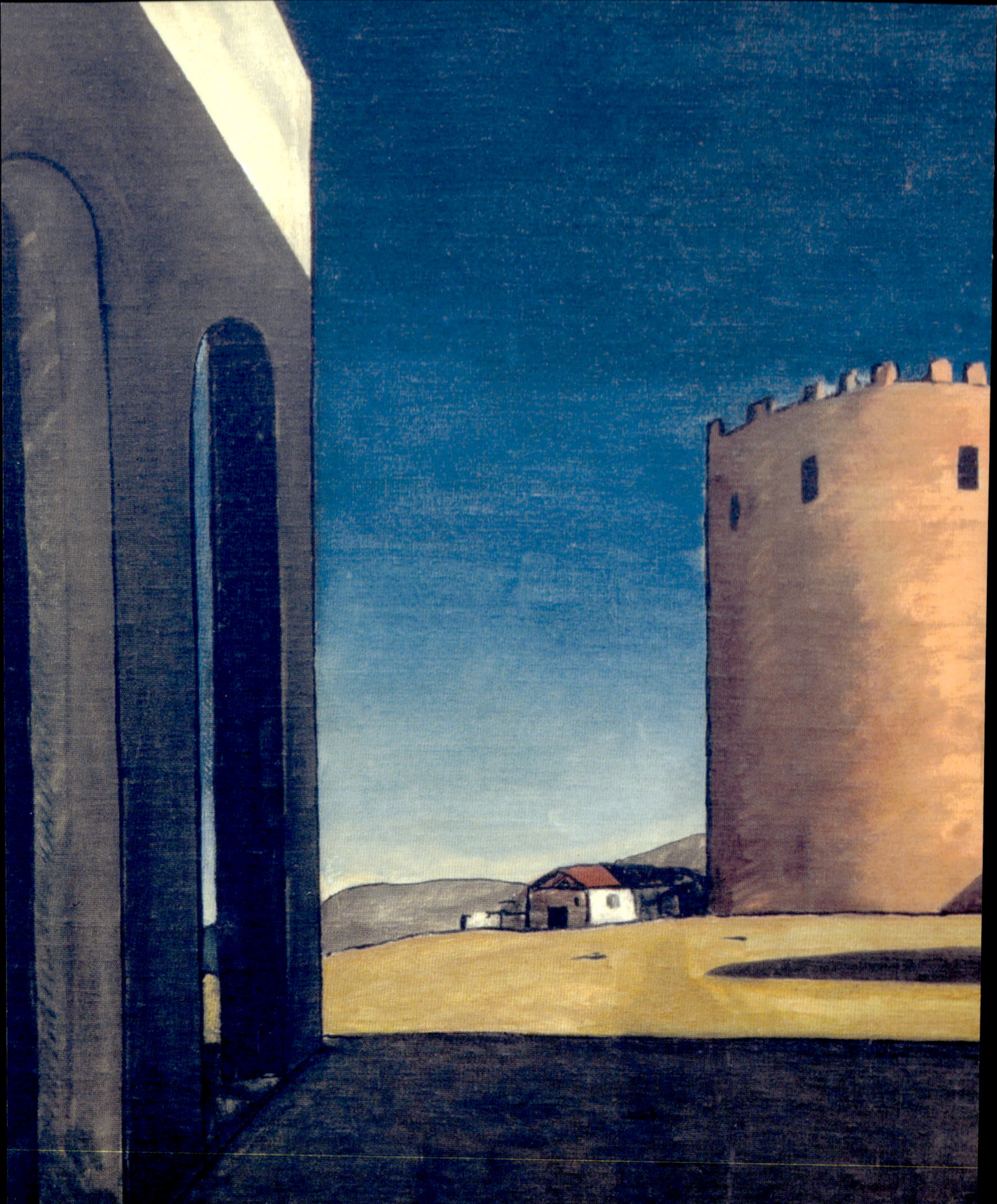

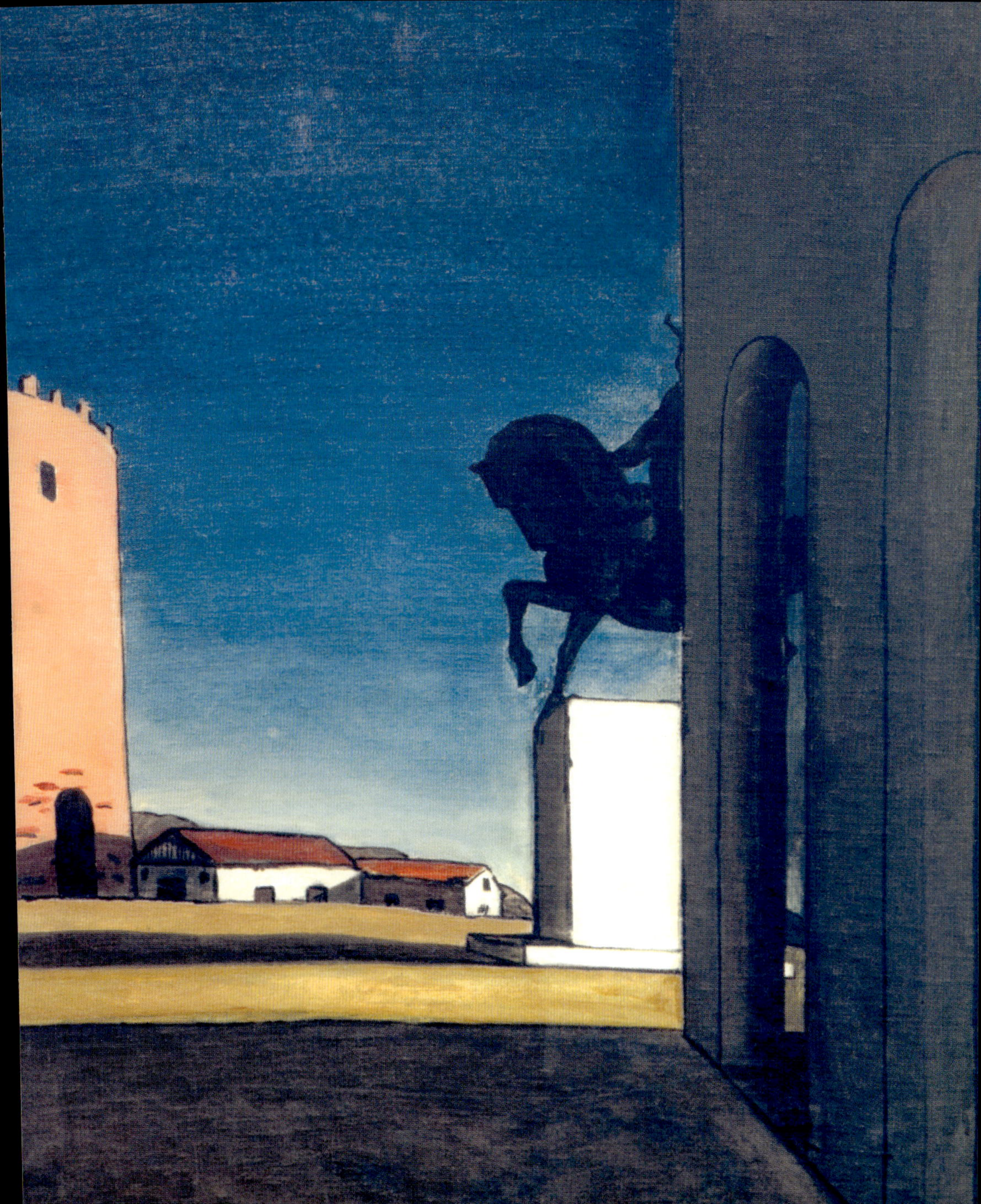

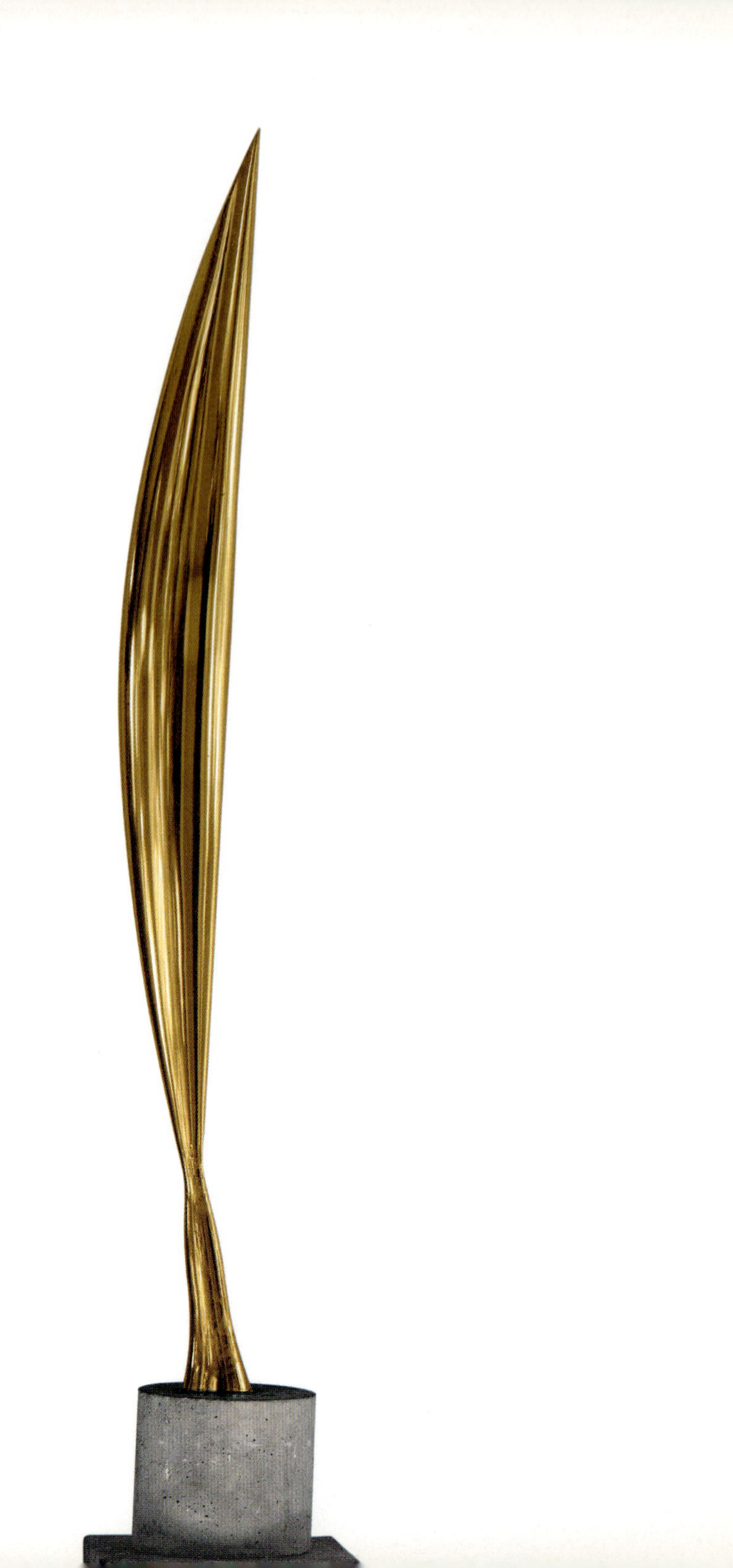

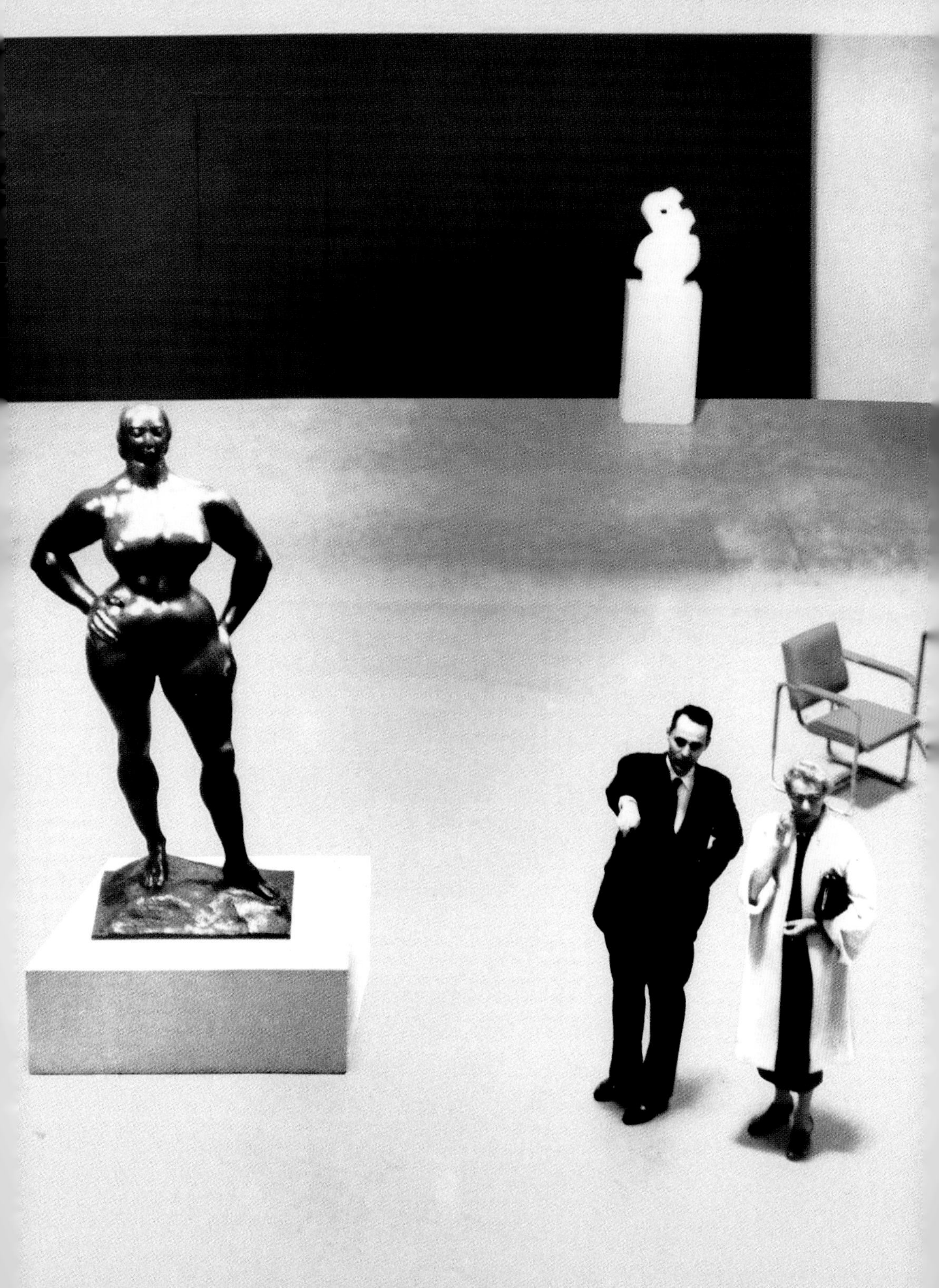

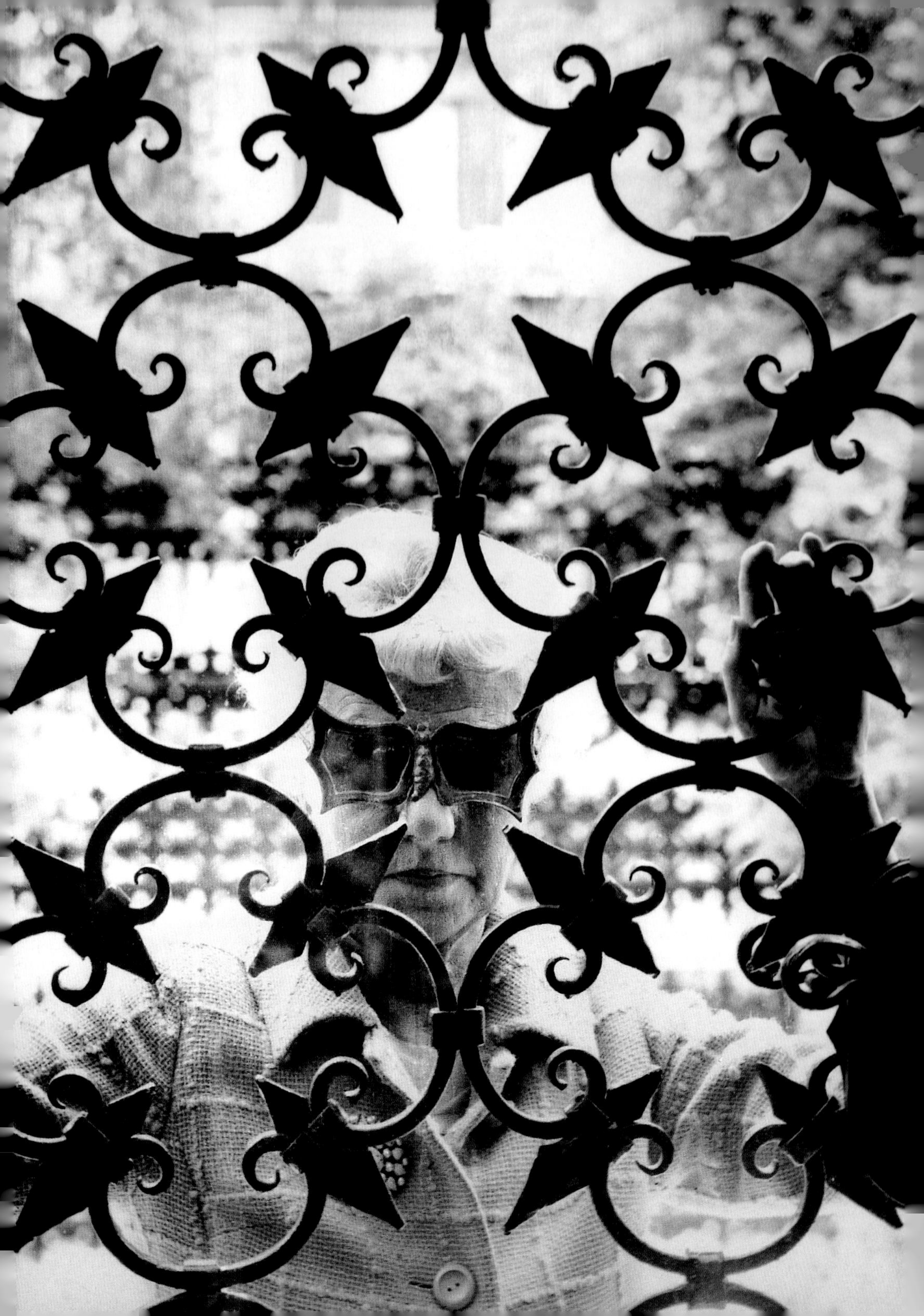

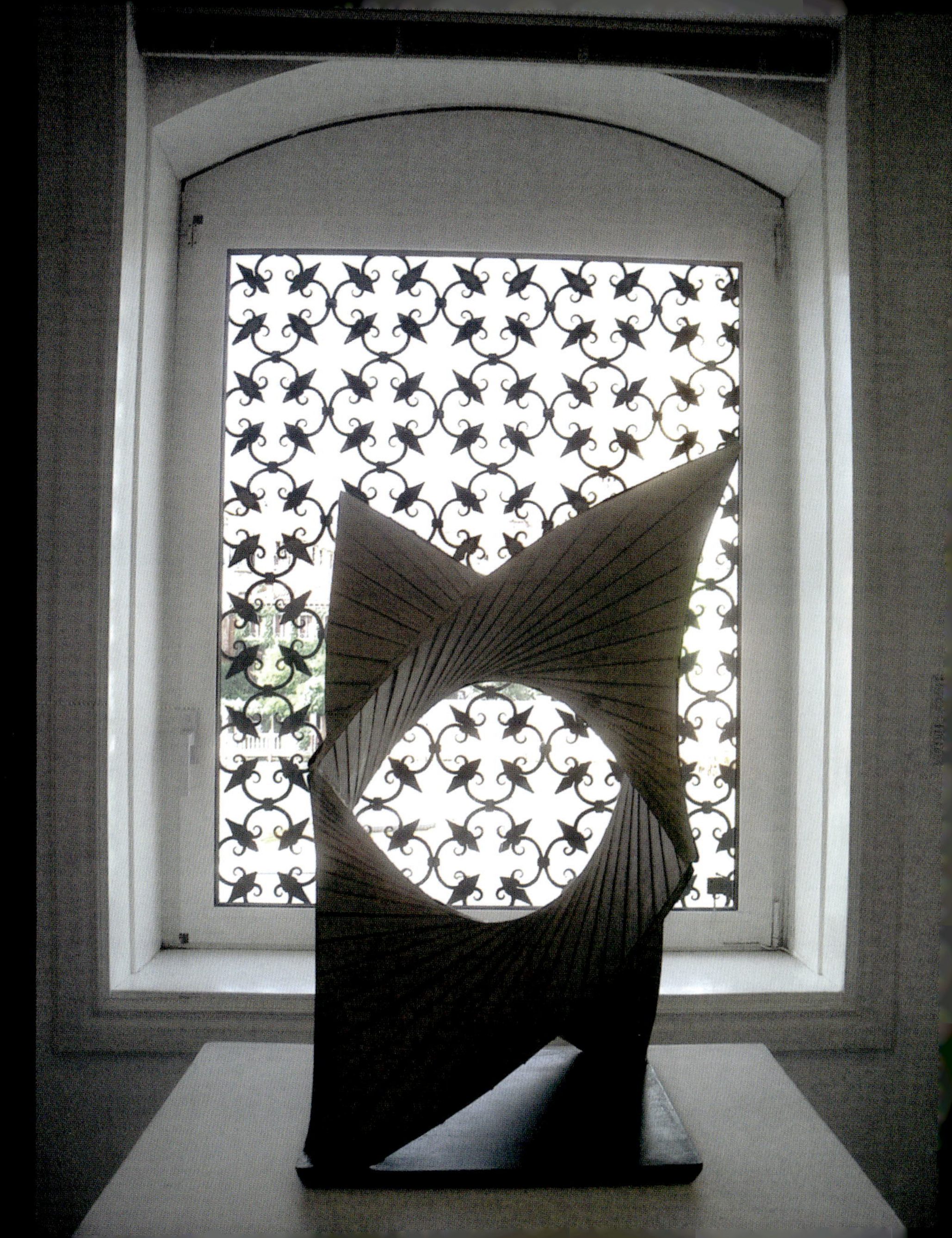

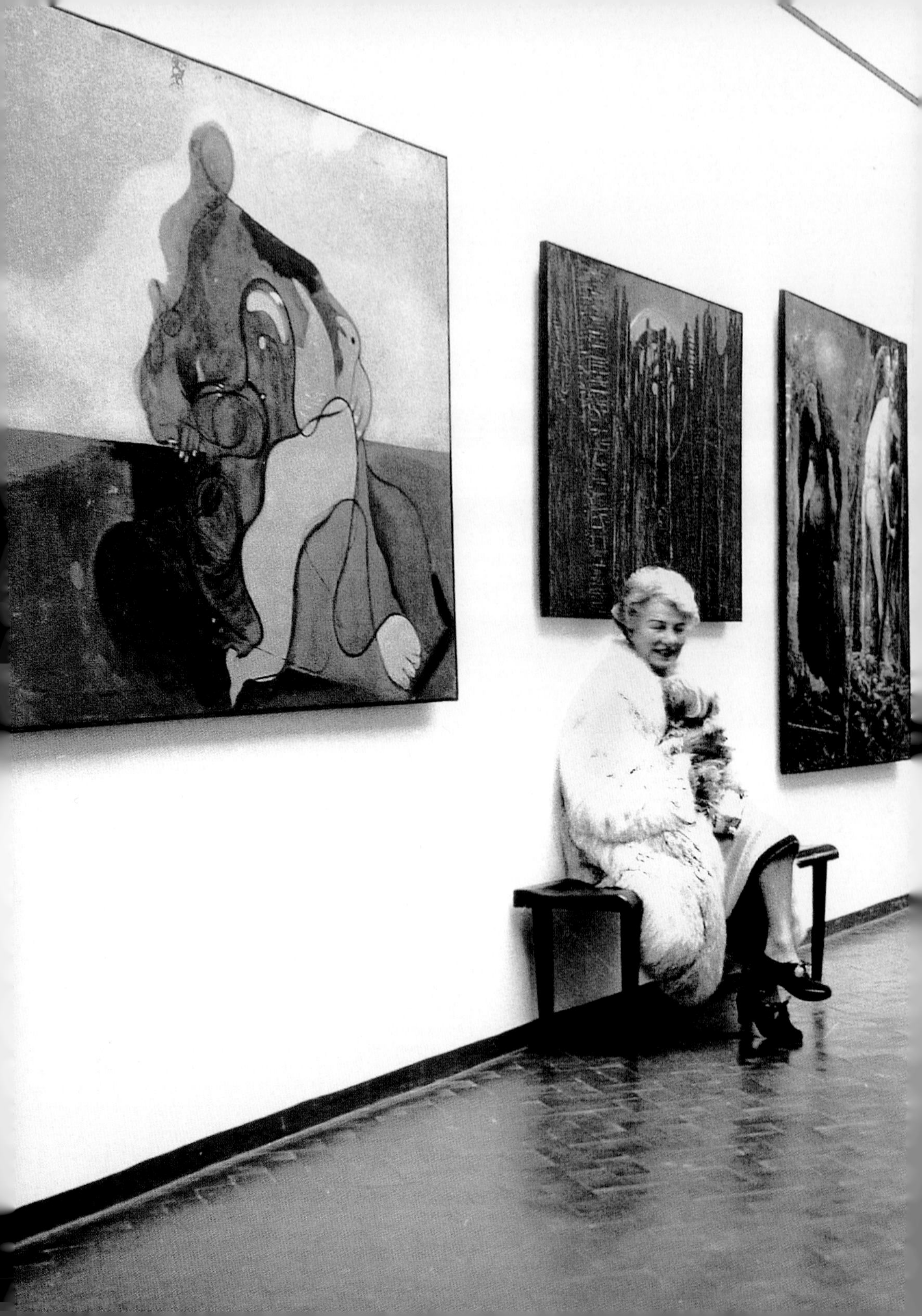

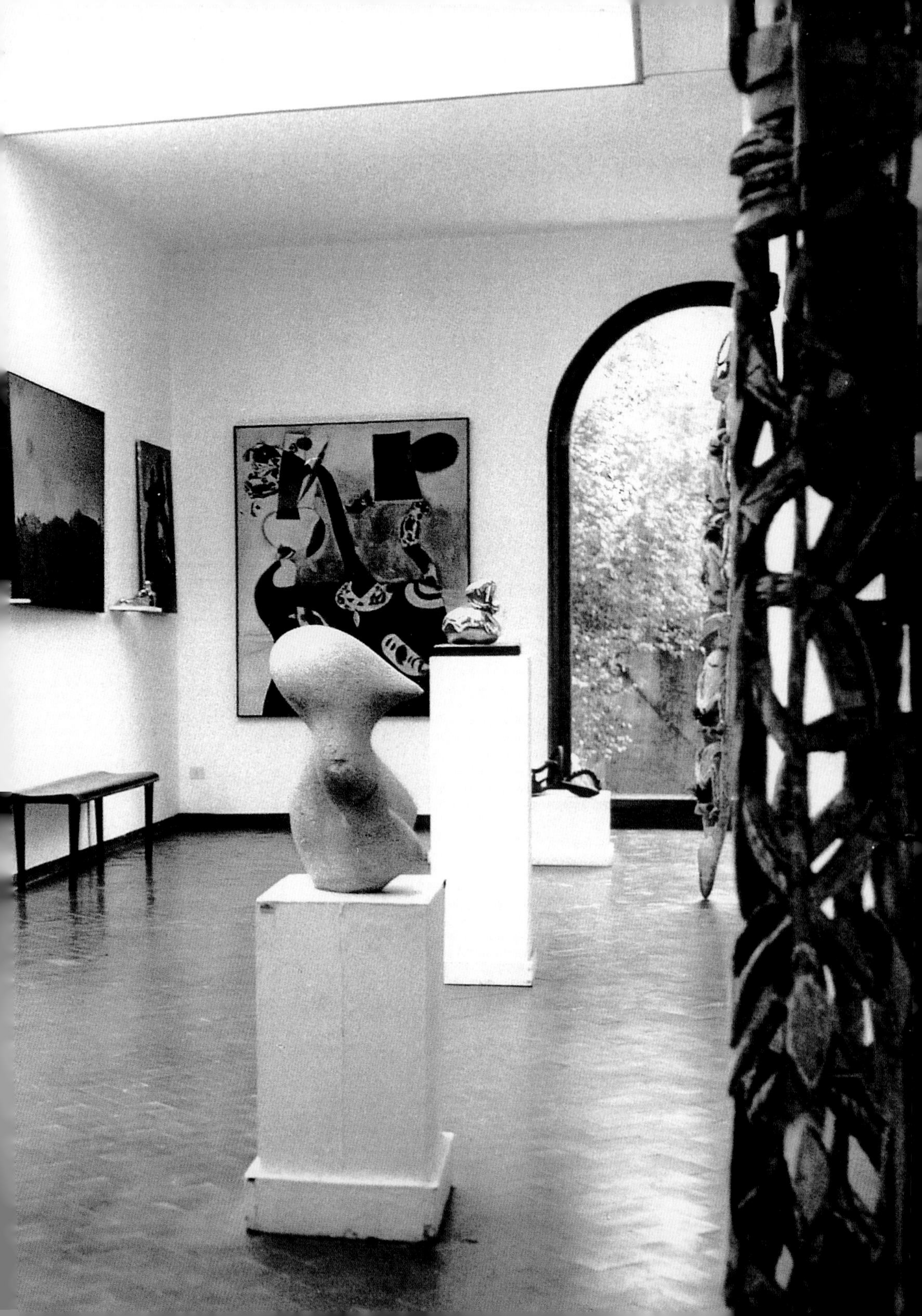

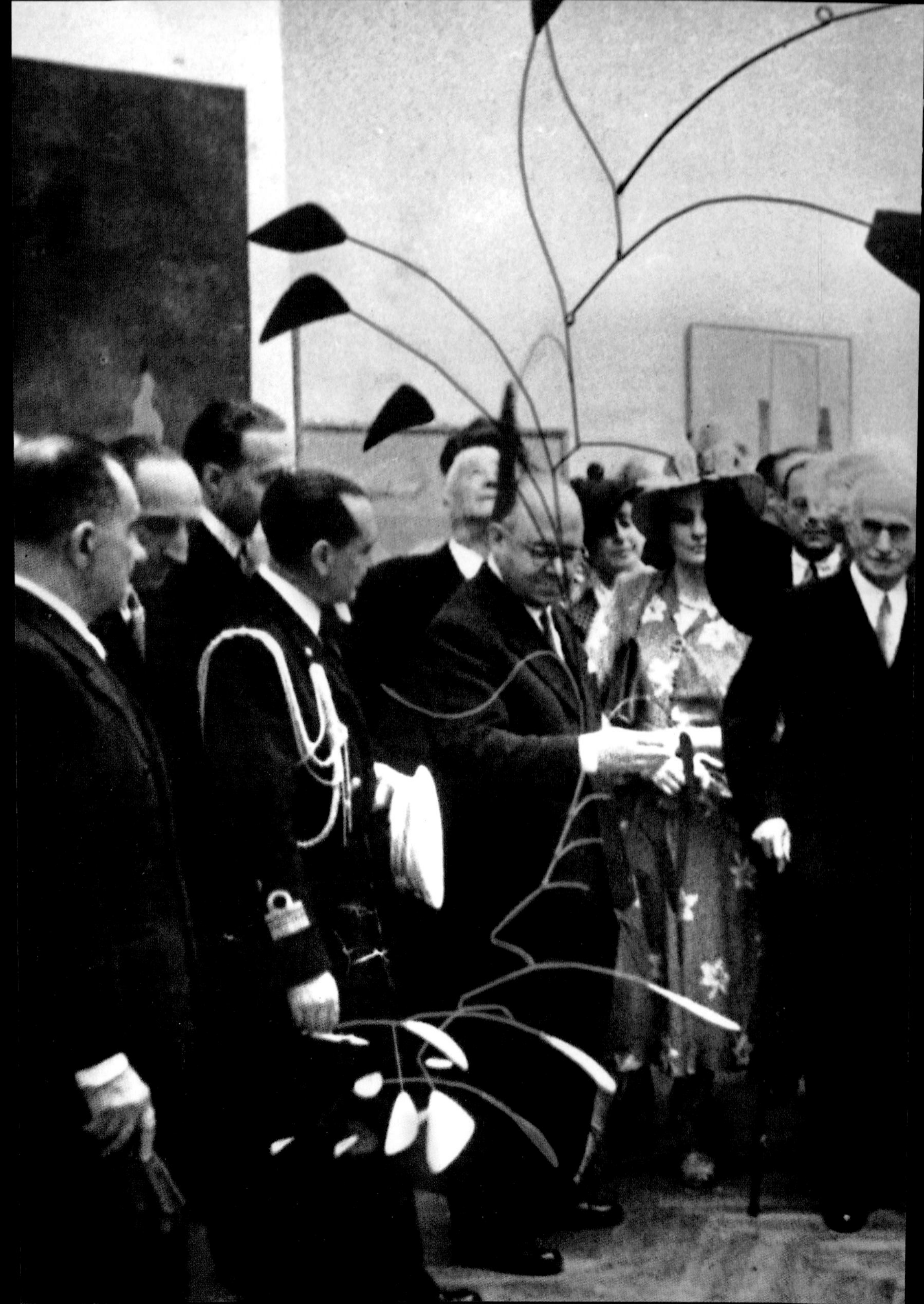

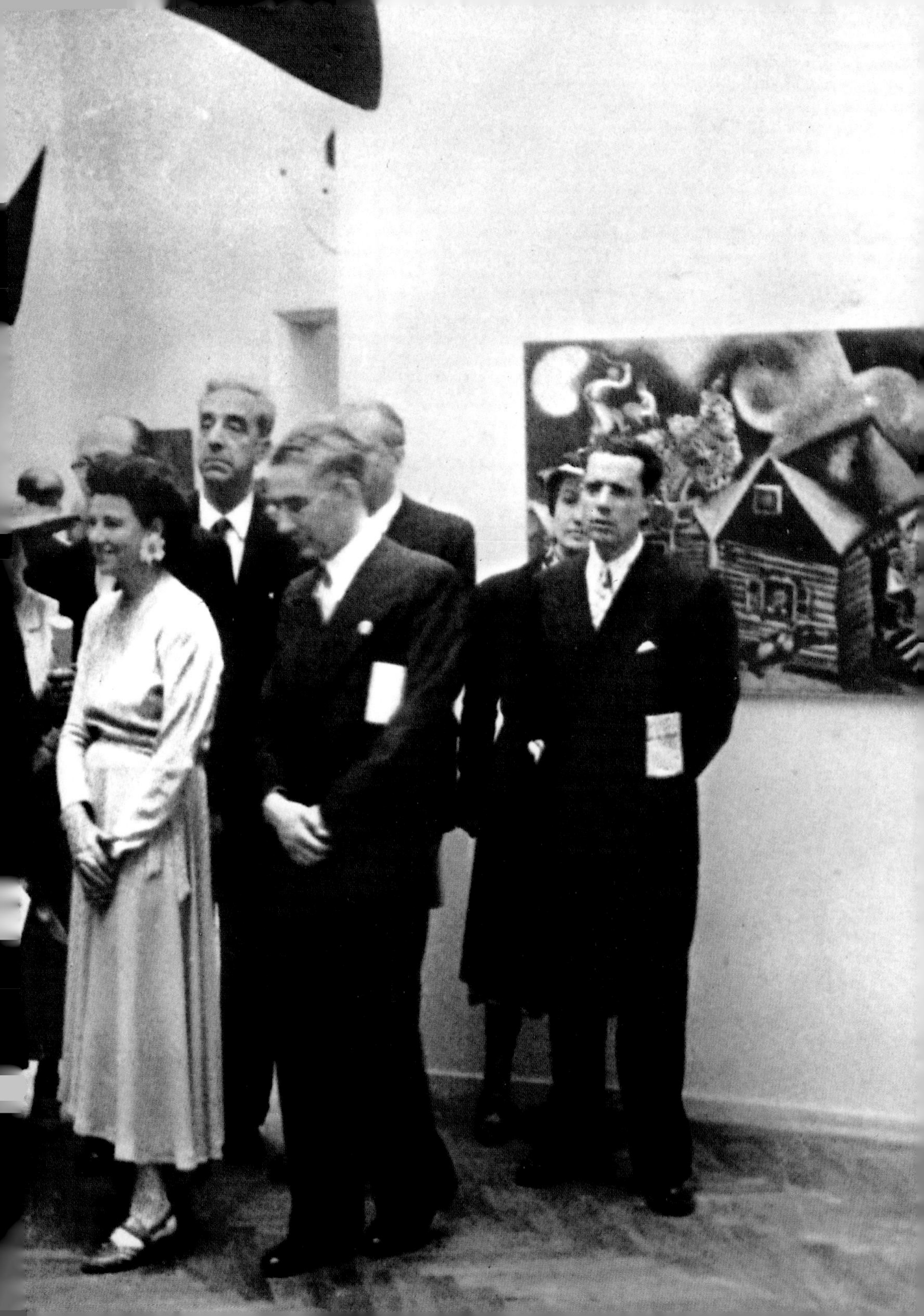

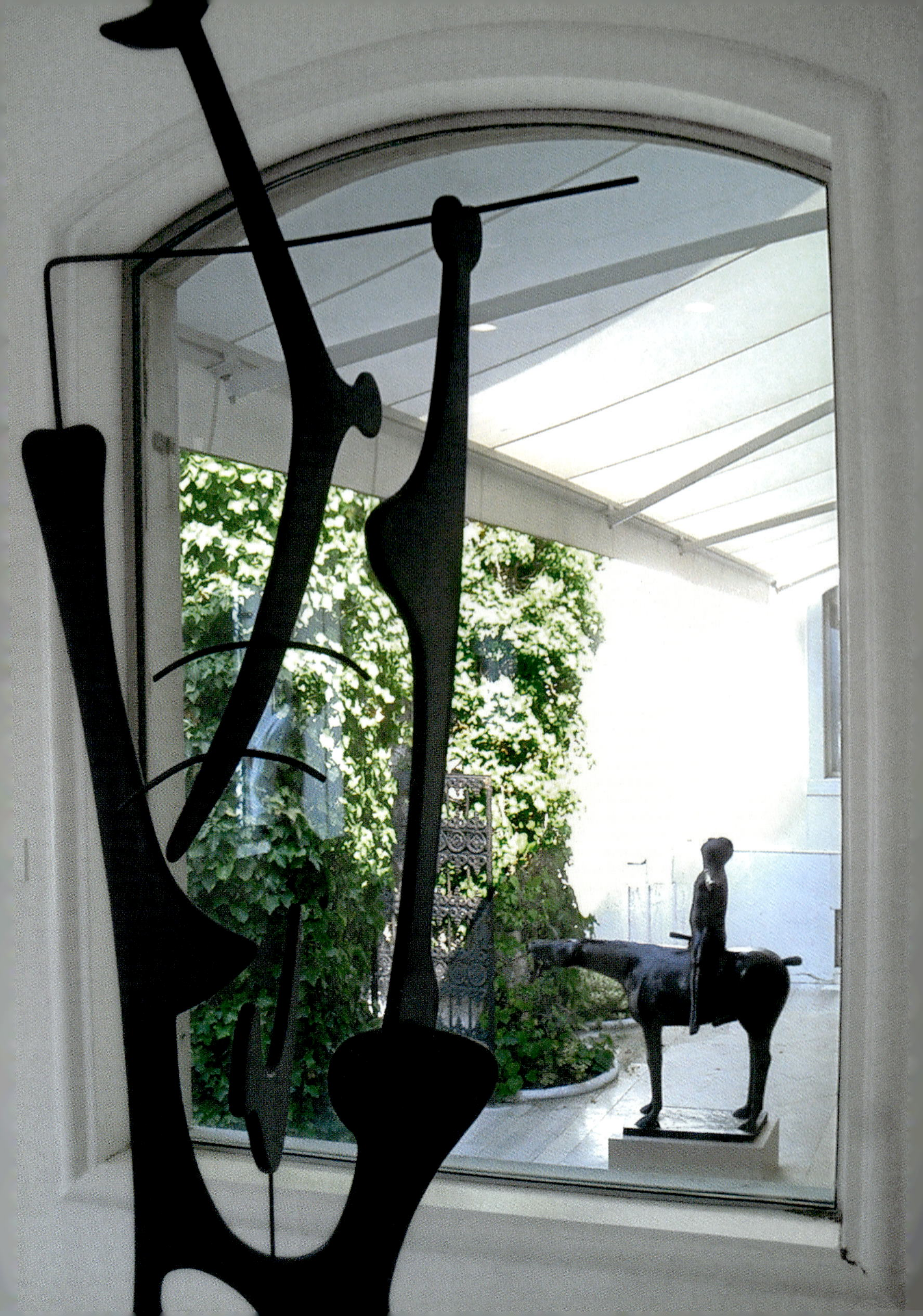

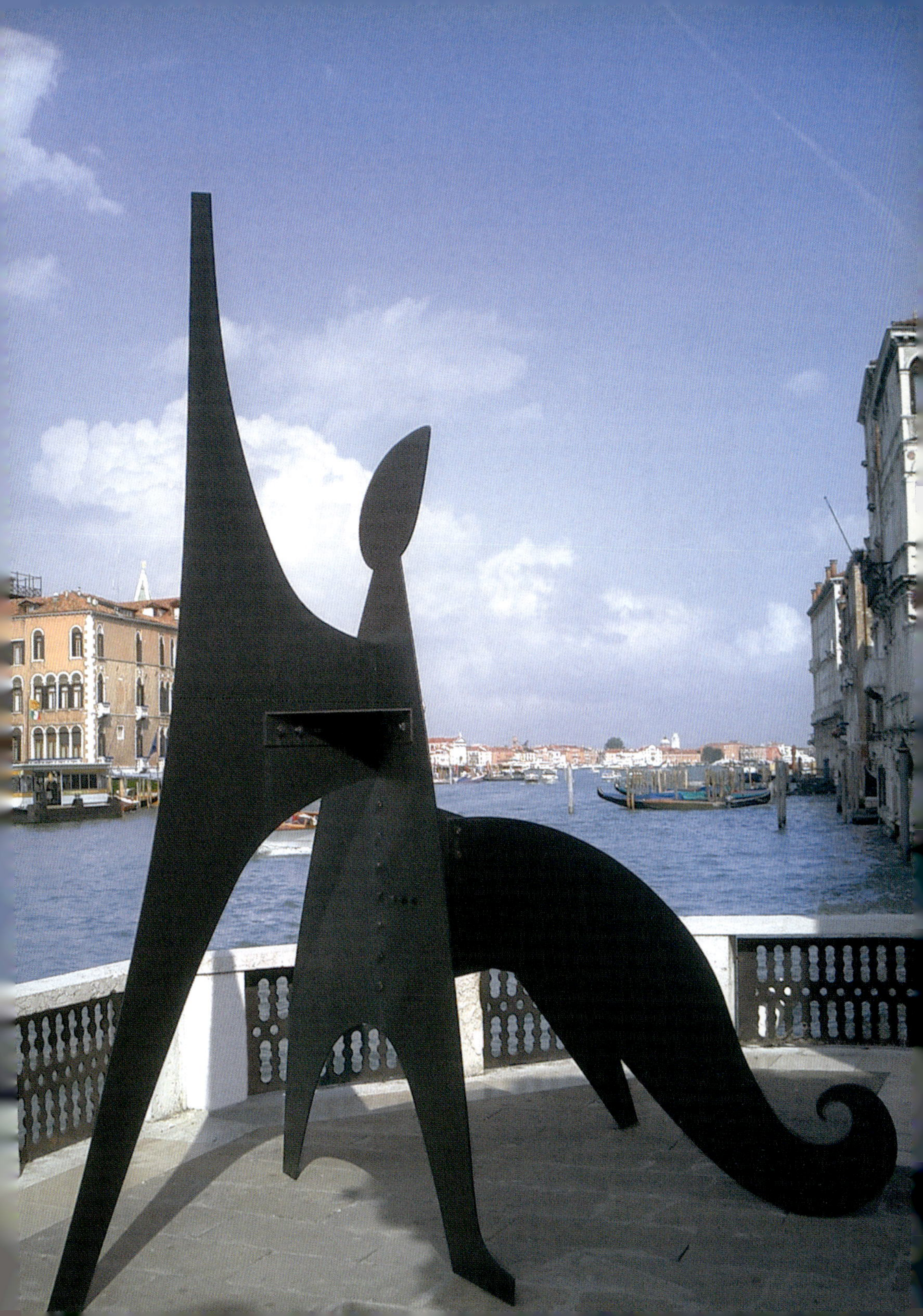

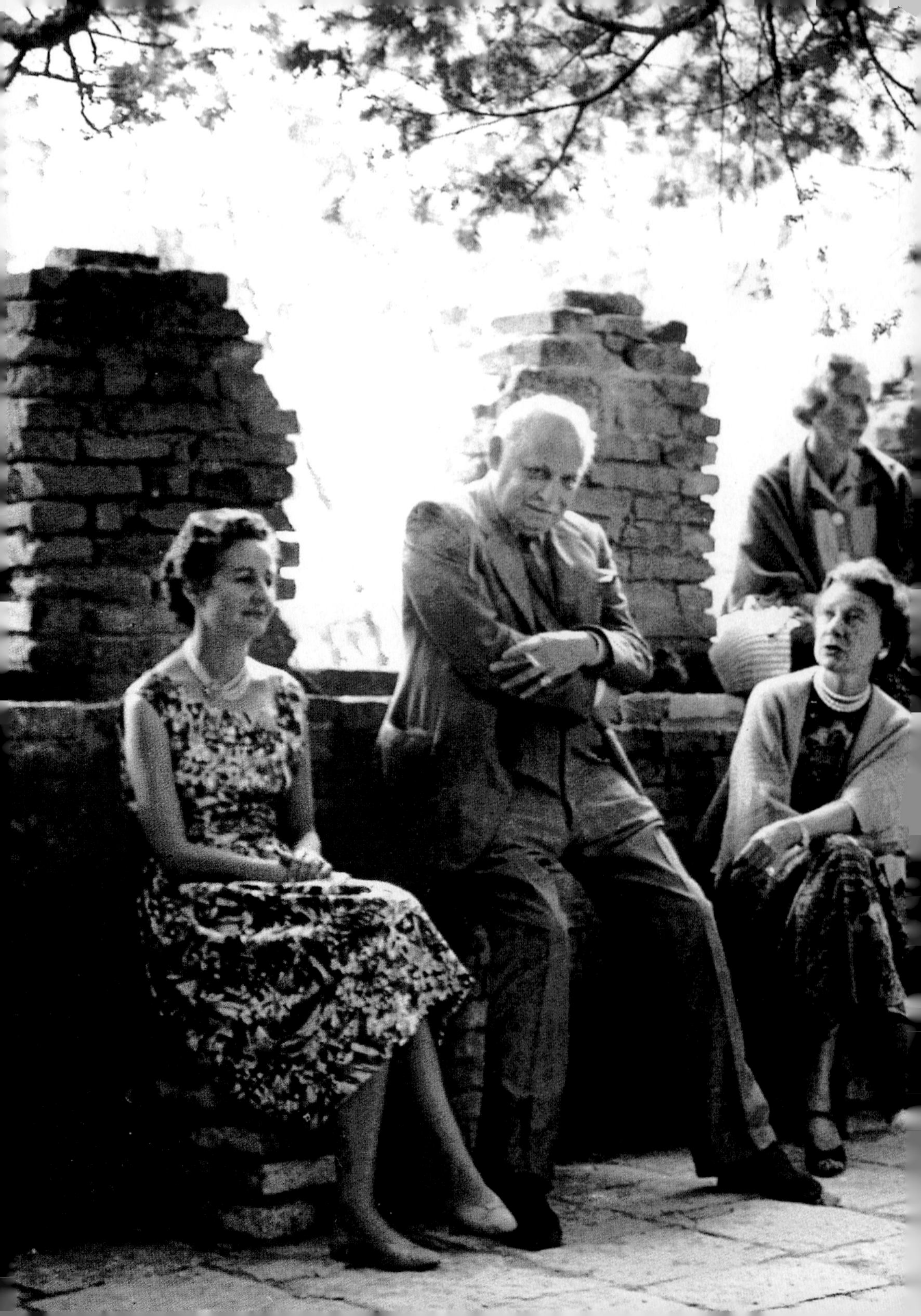

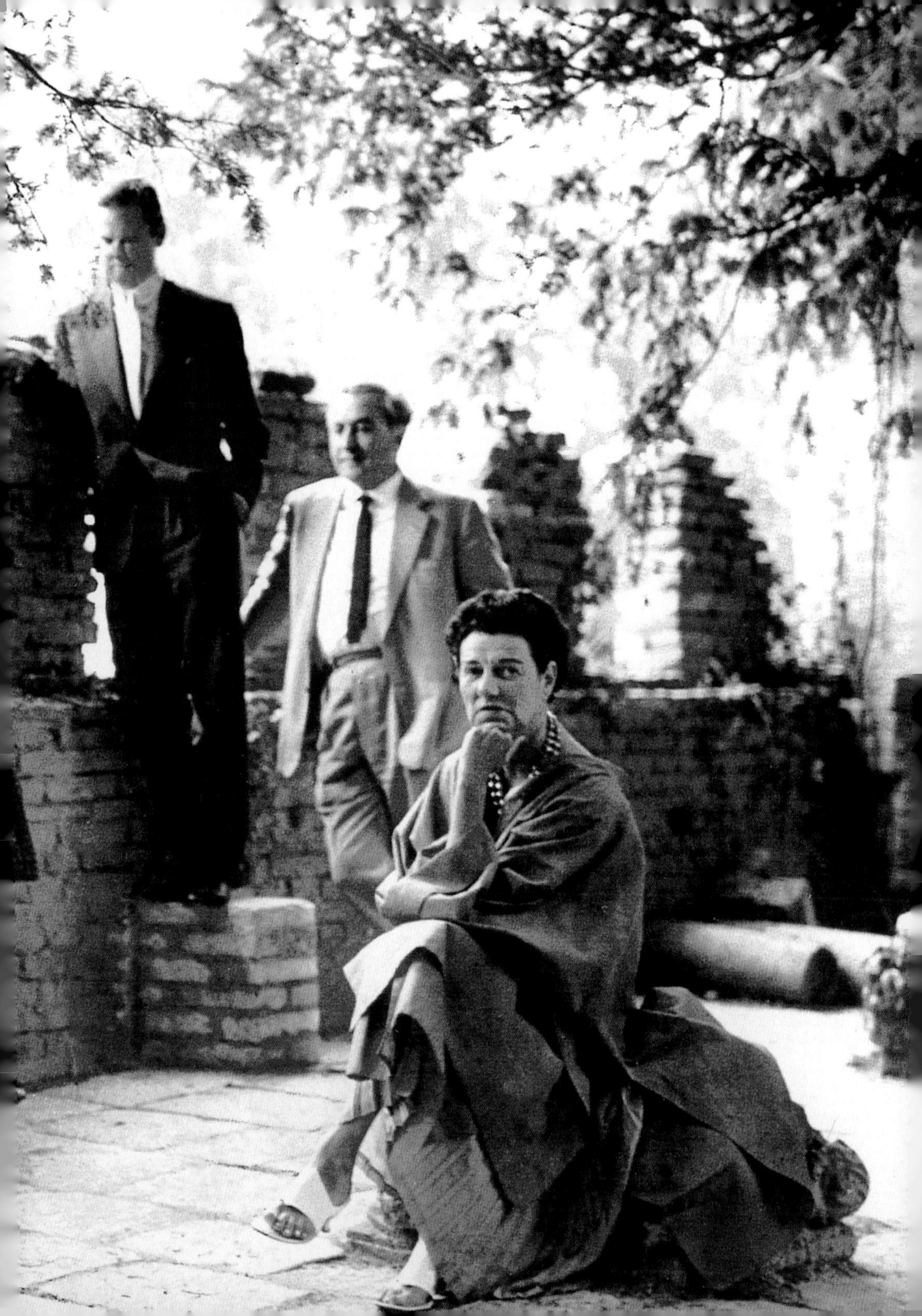

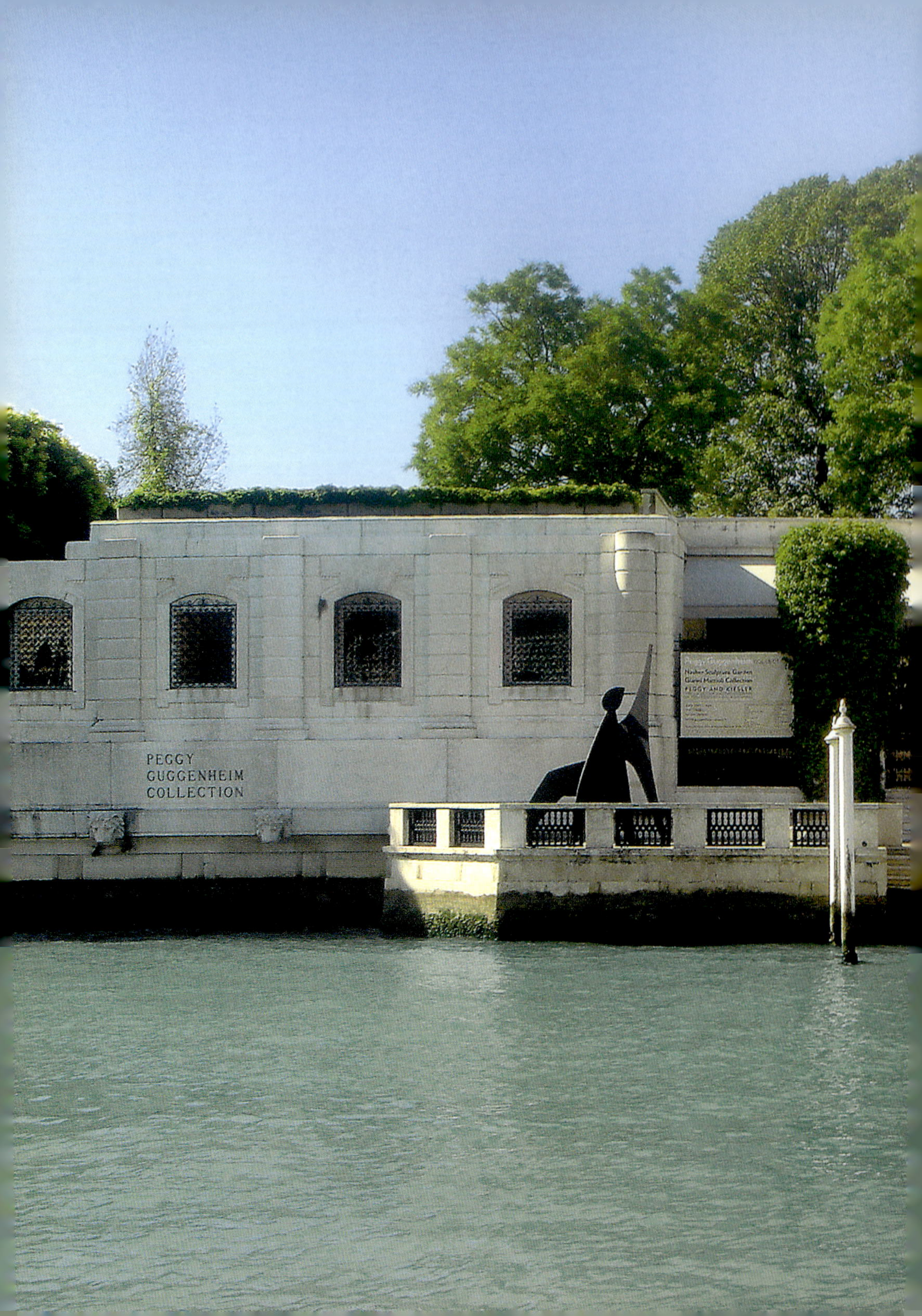

PEGGY
GUGGENHEIM
COLLECTION

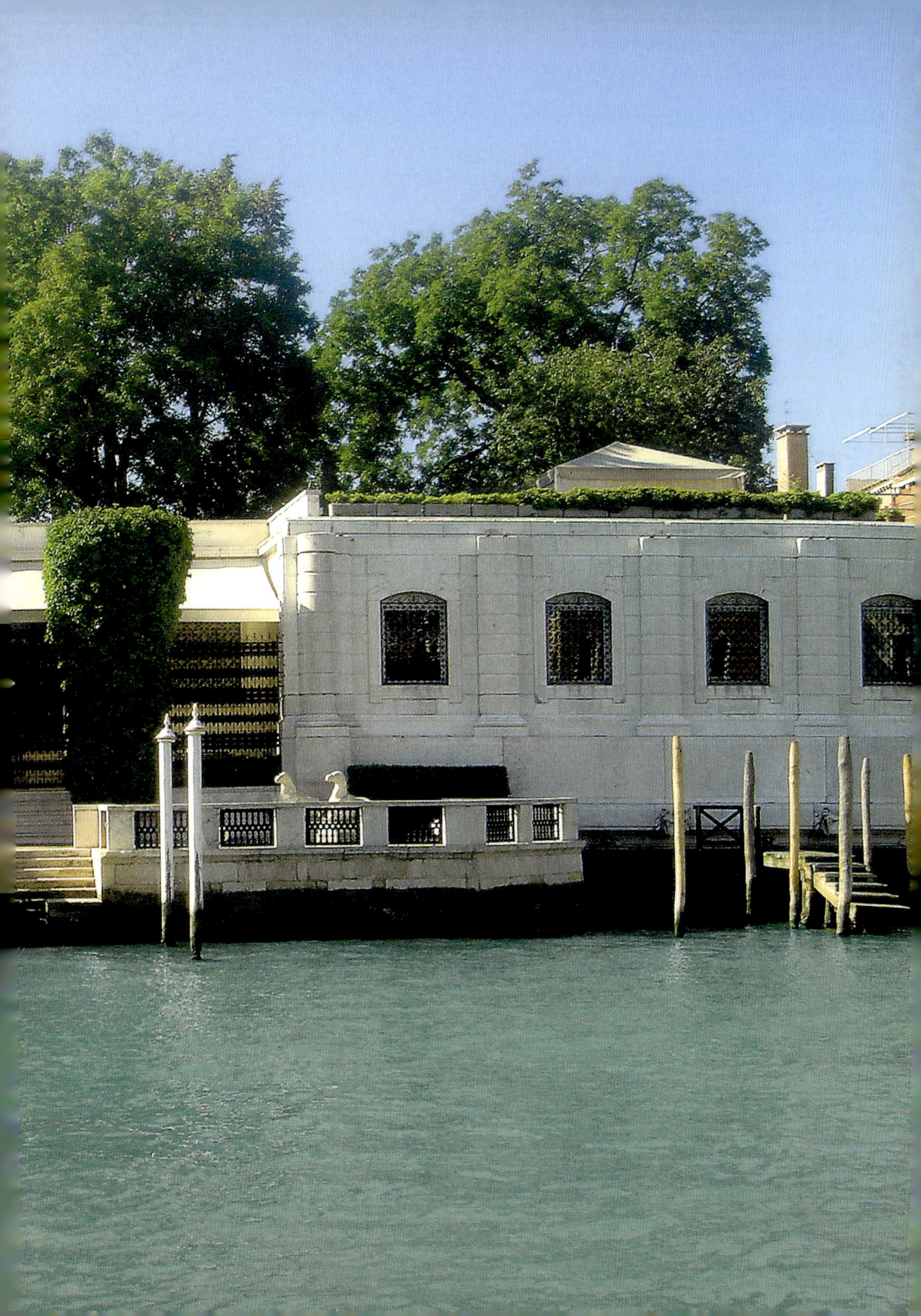

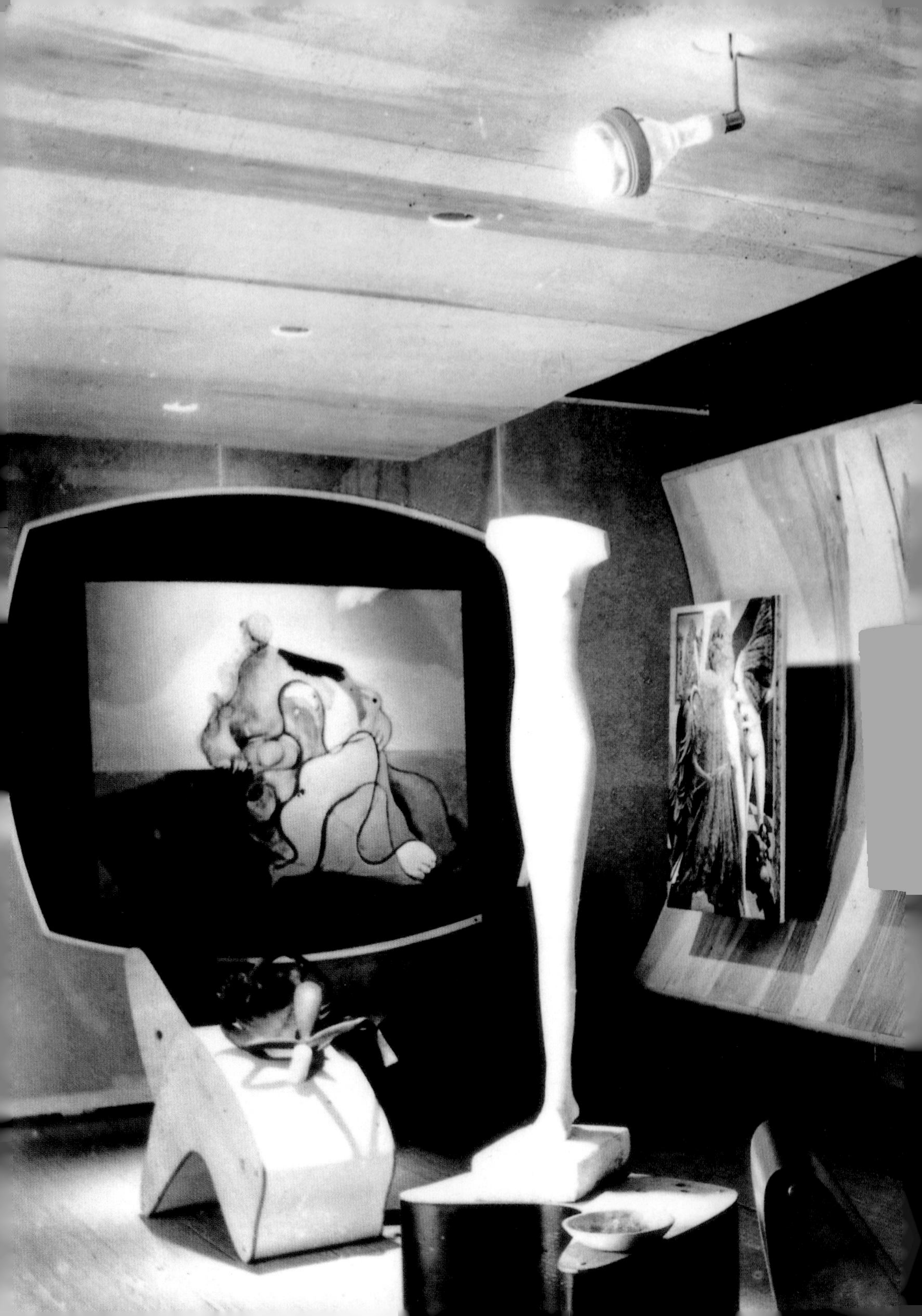

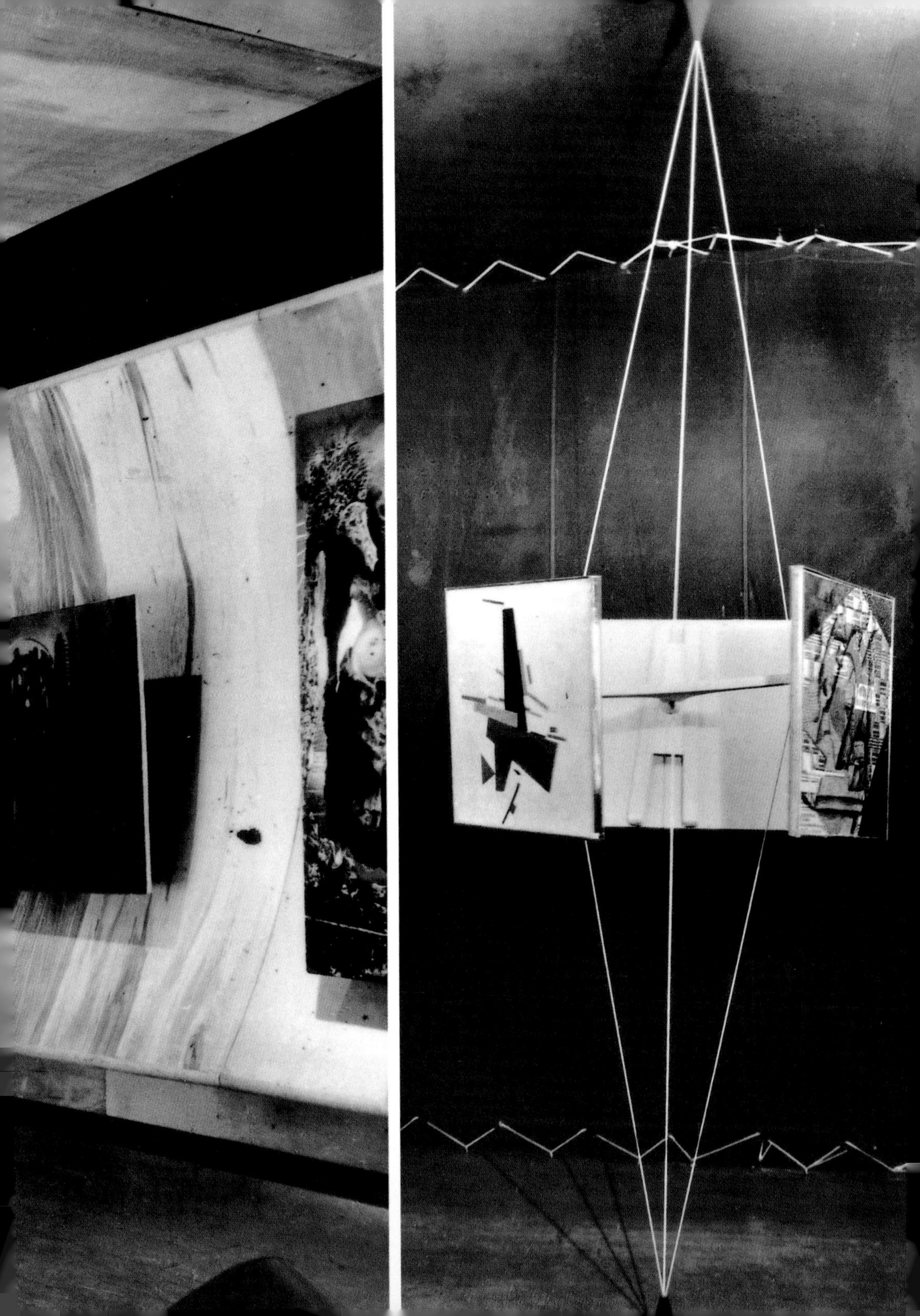

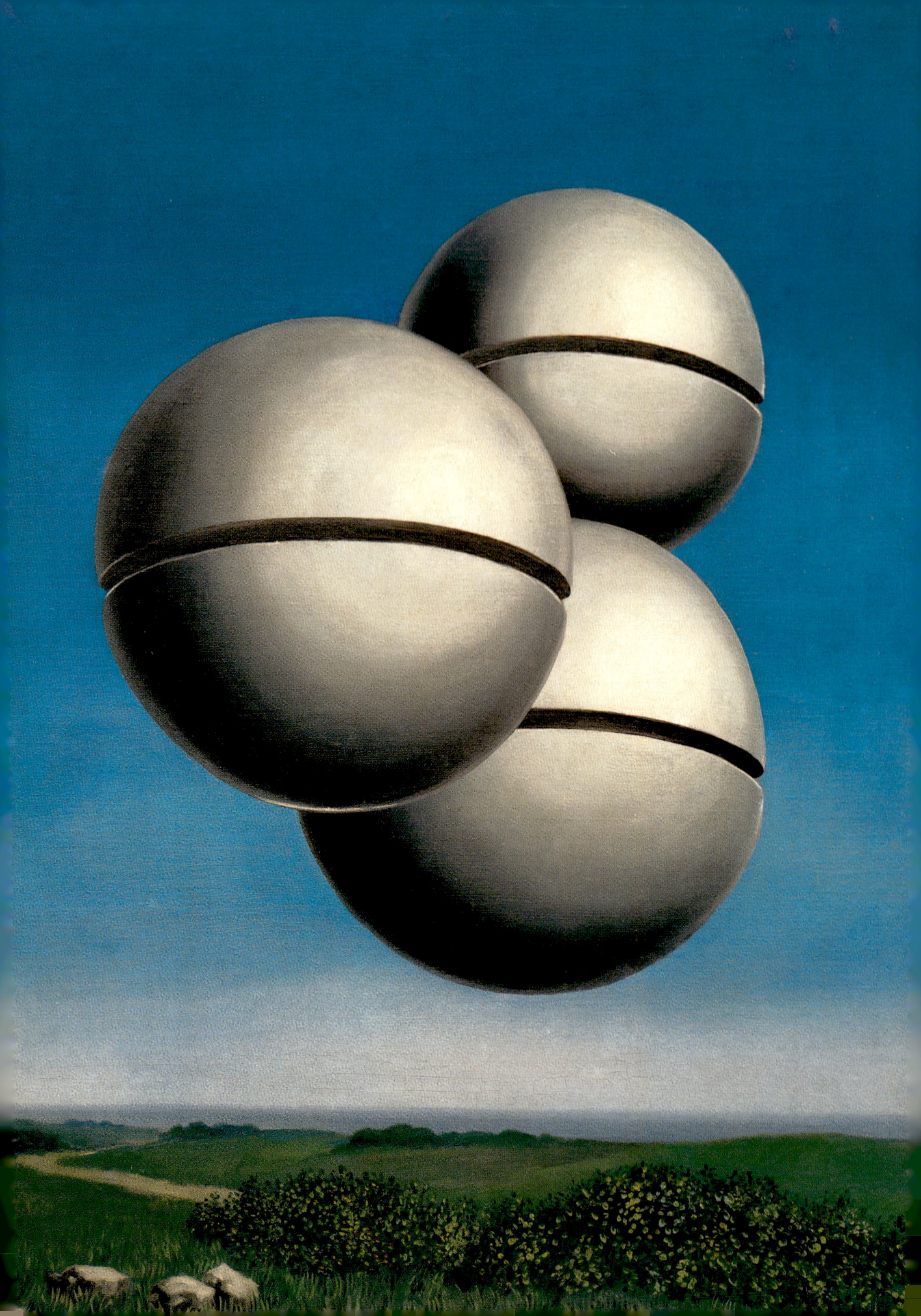

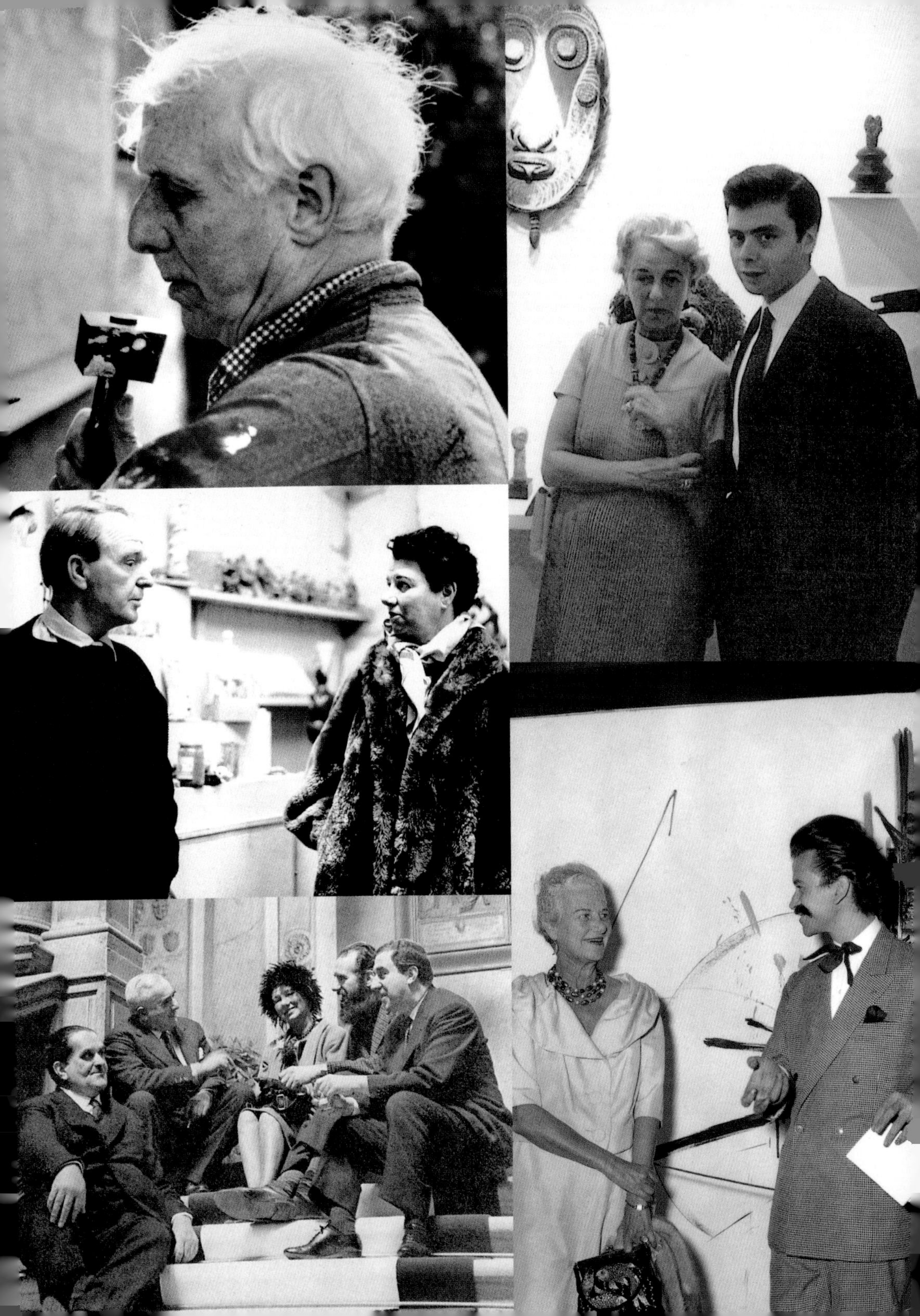

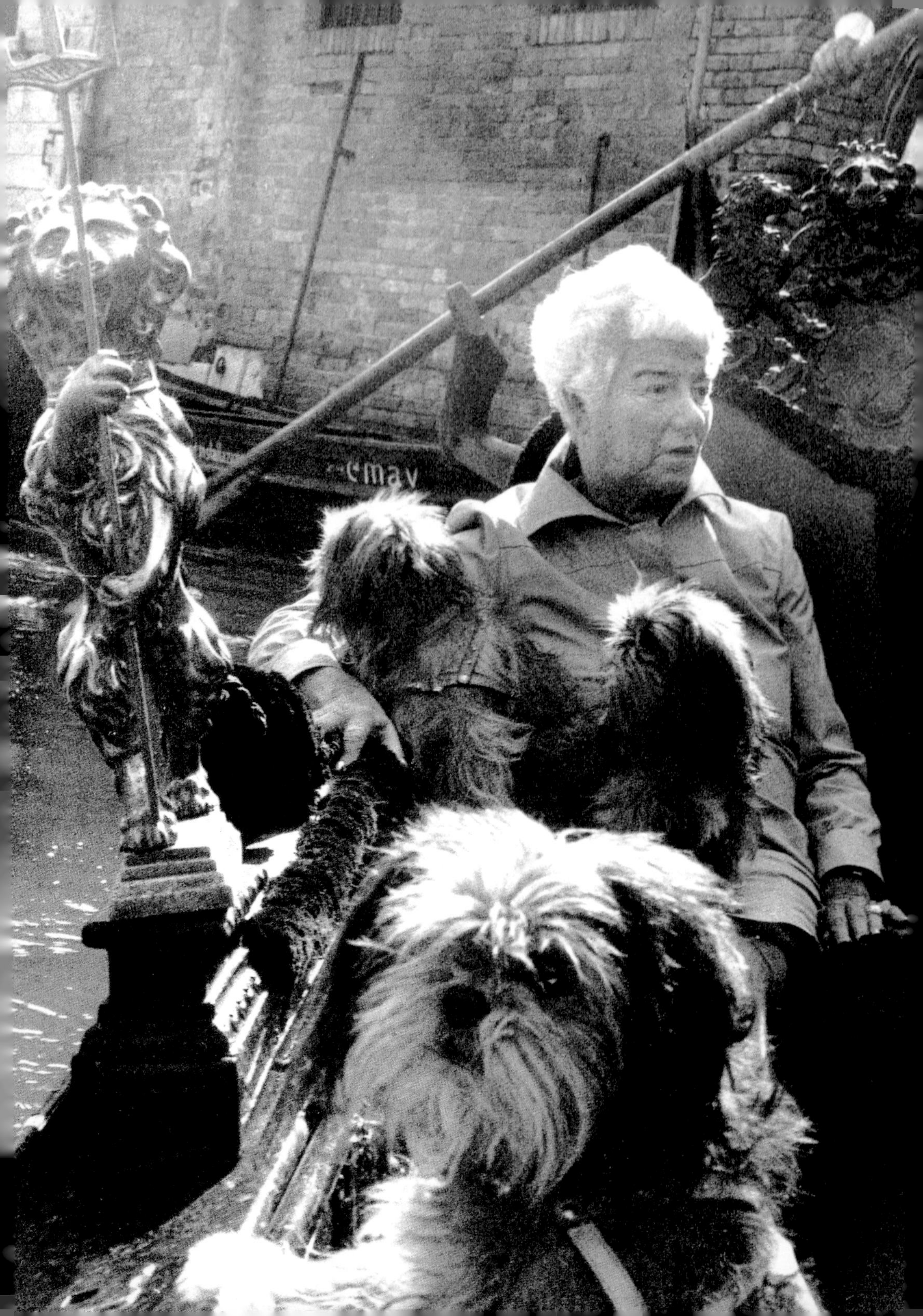

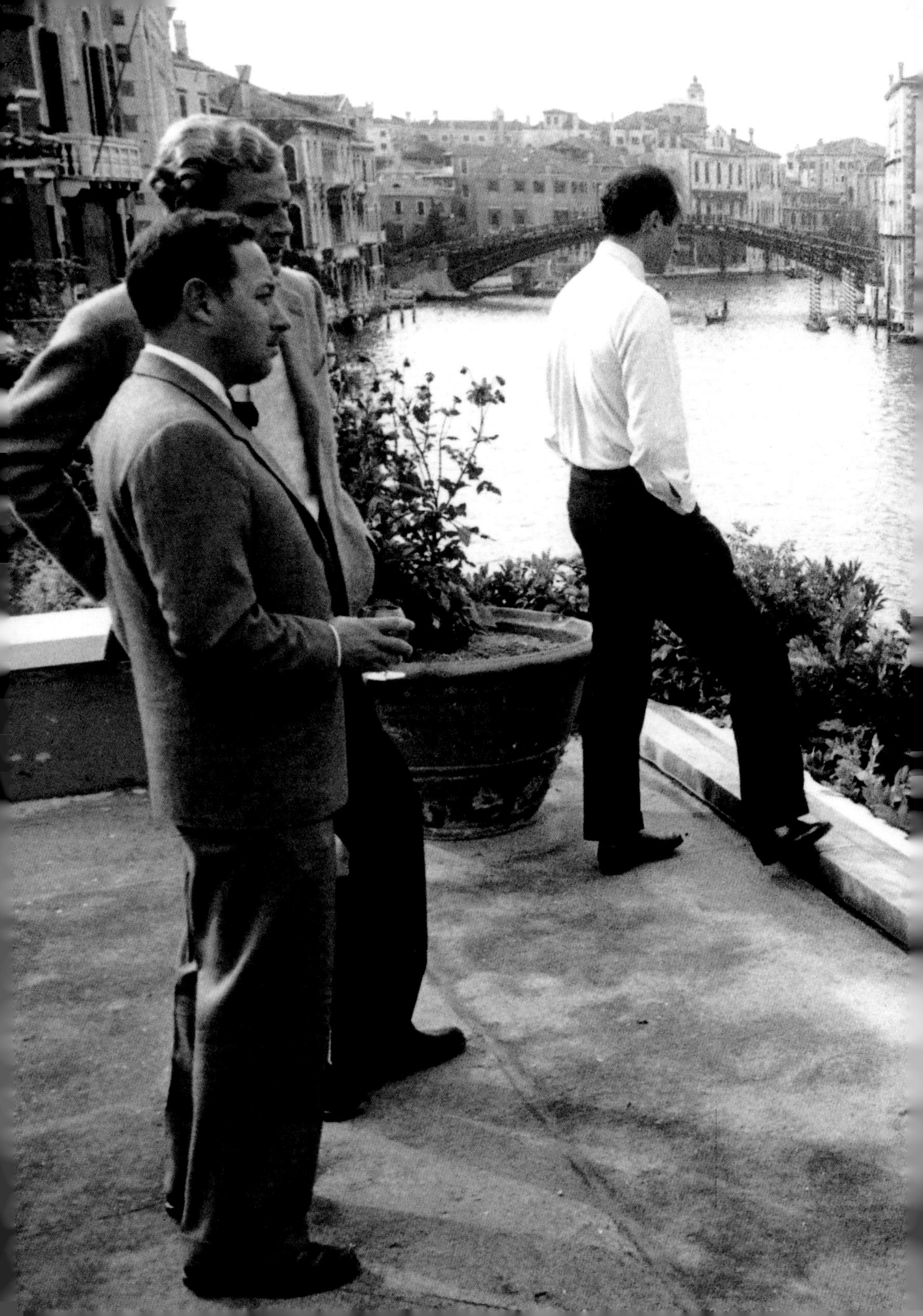

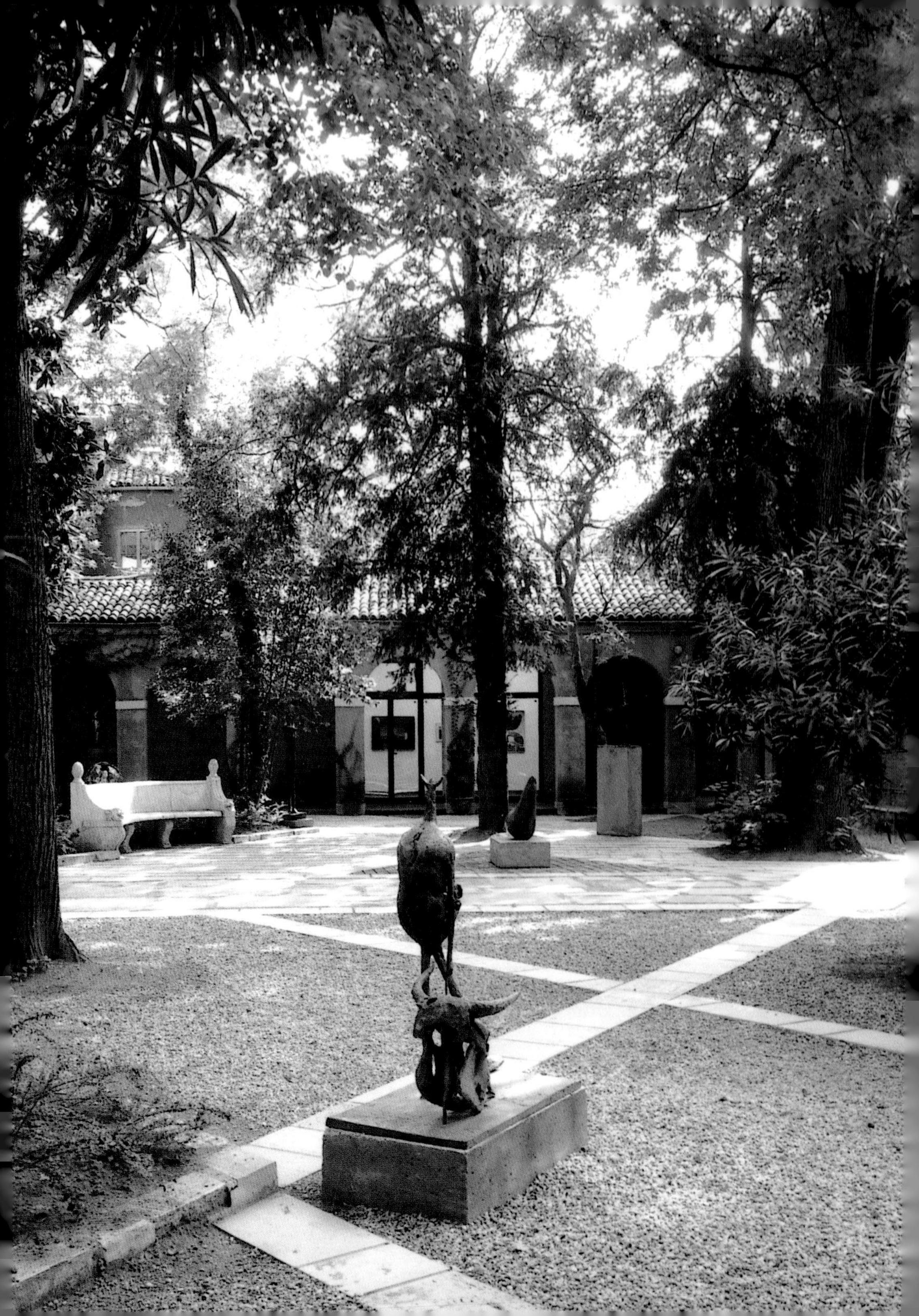

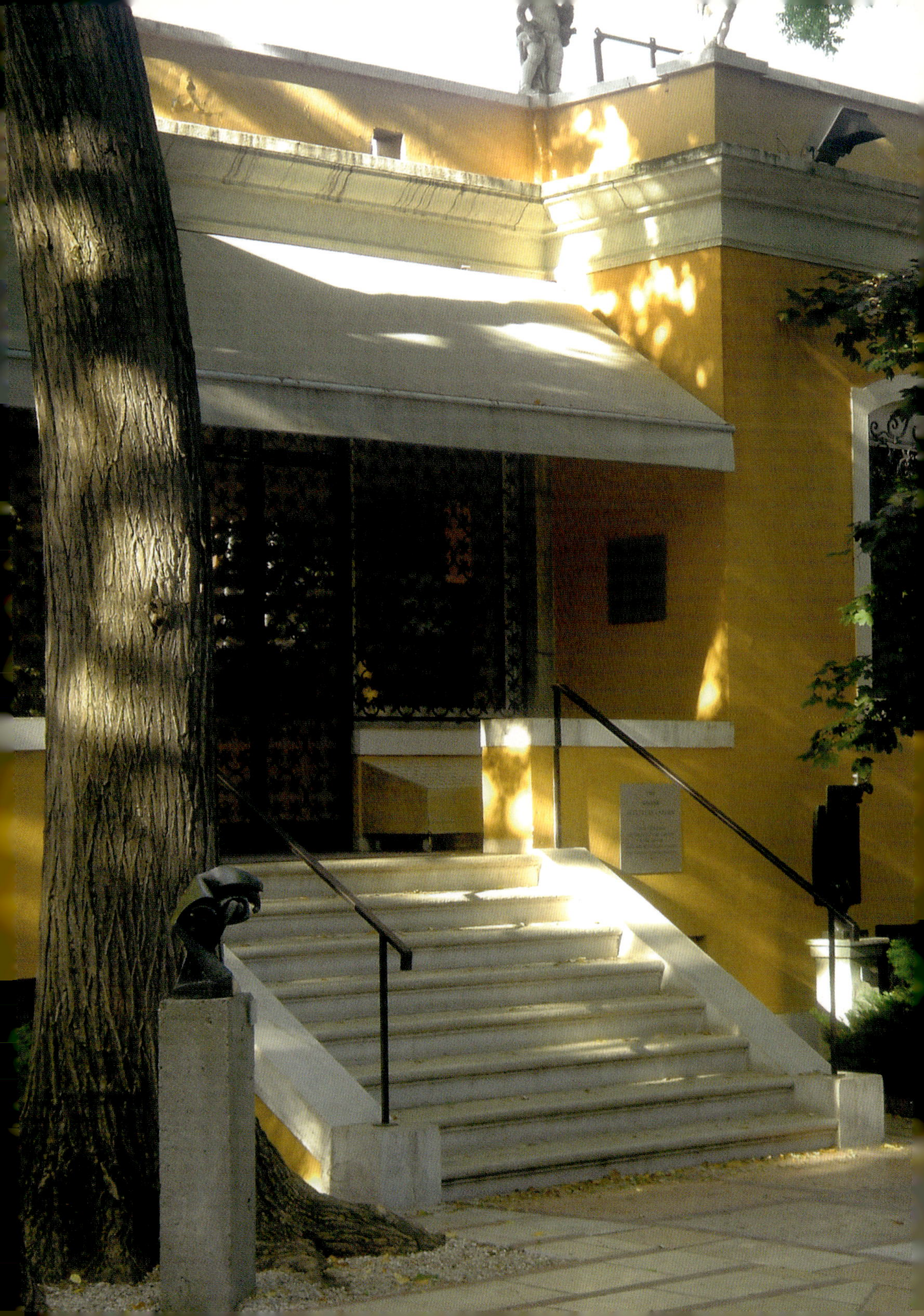

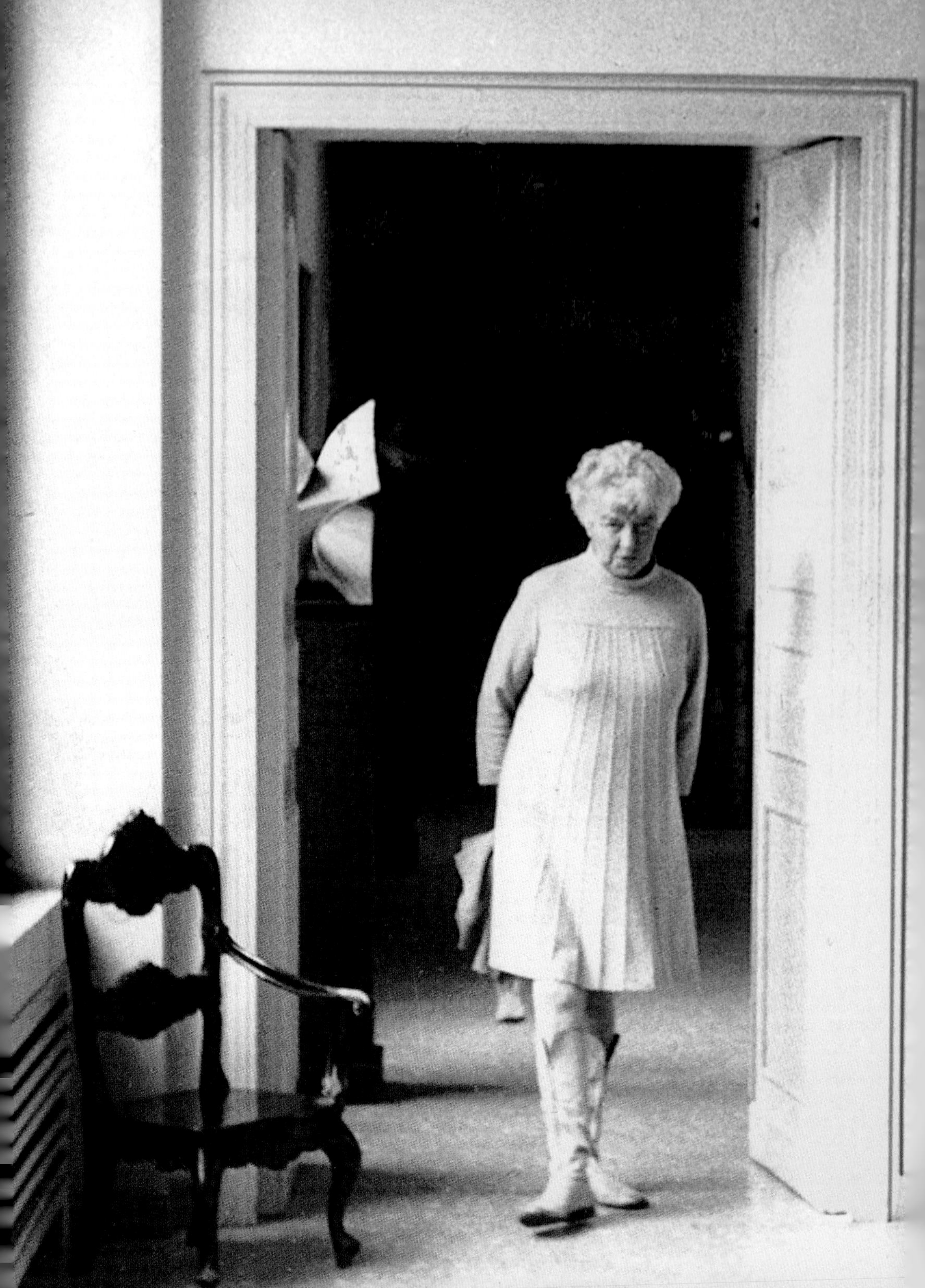

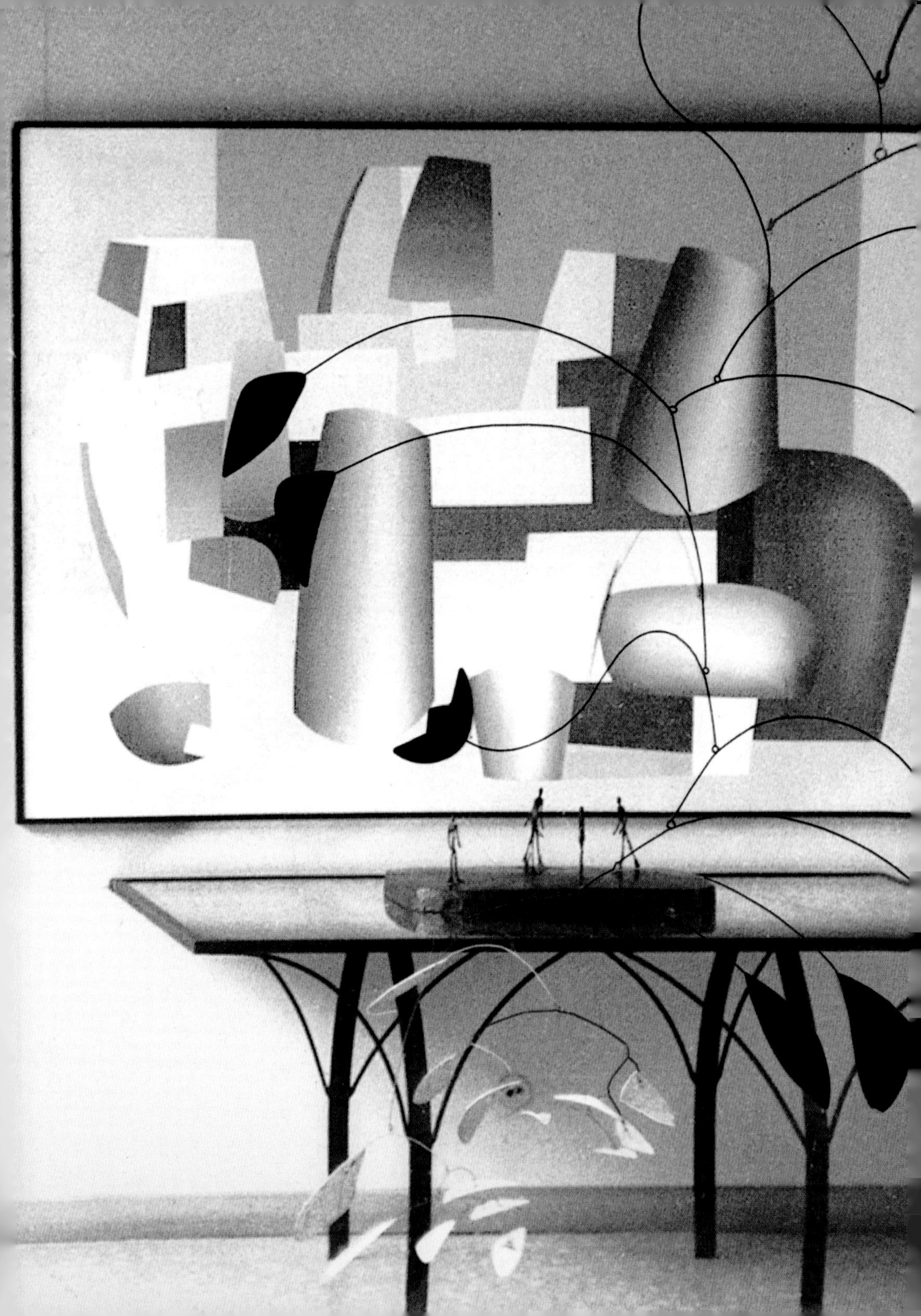

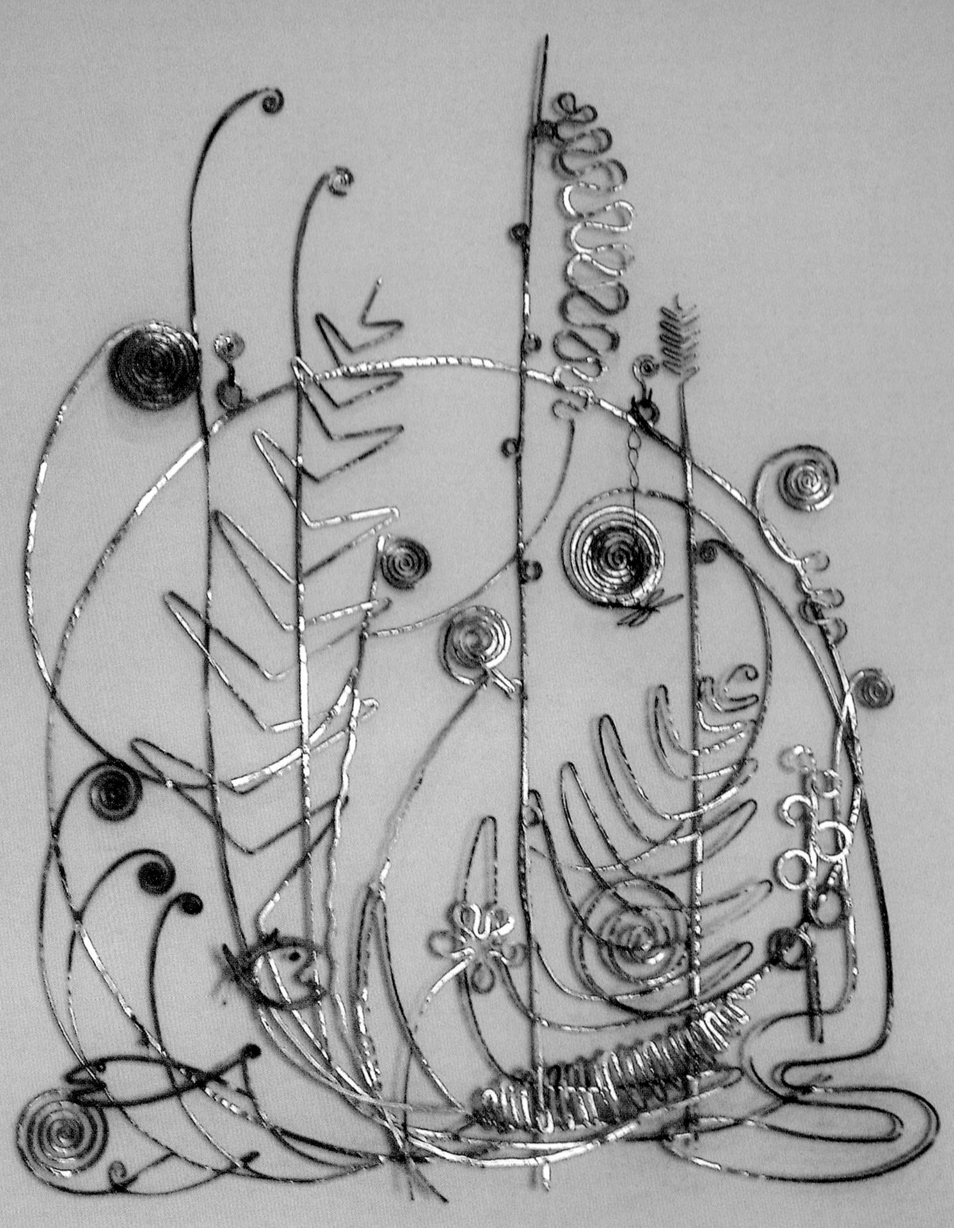

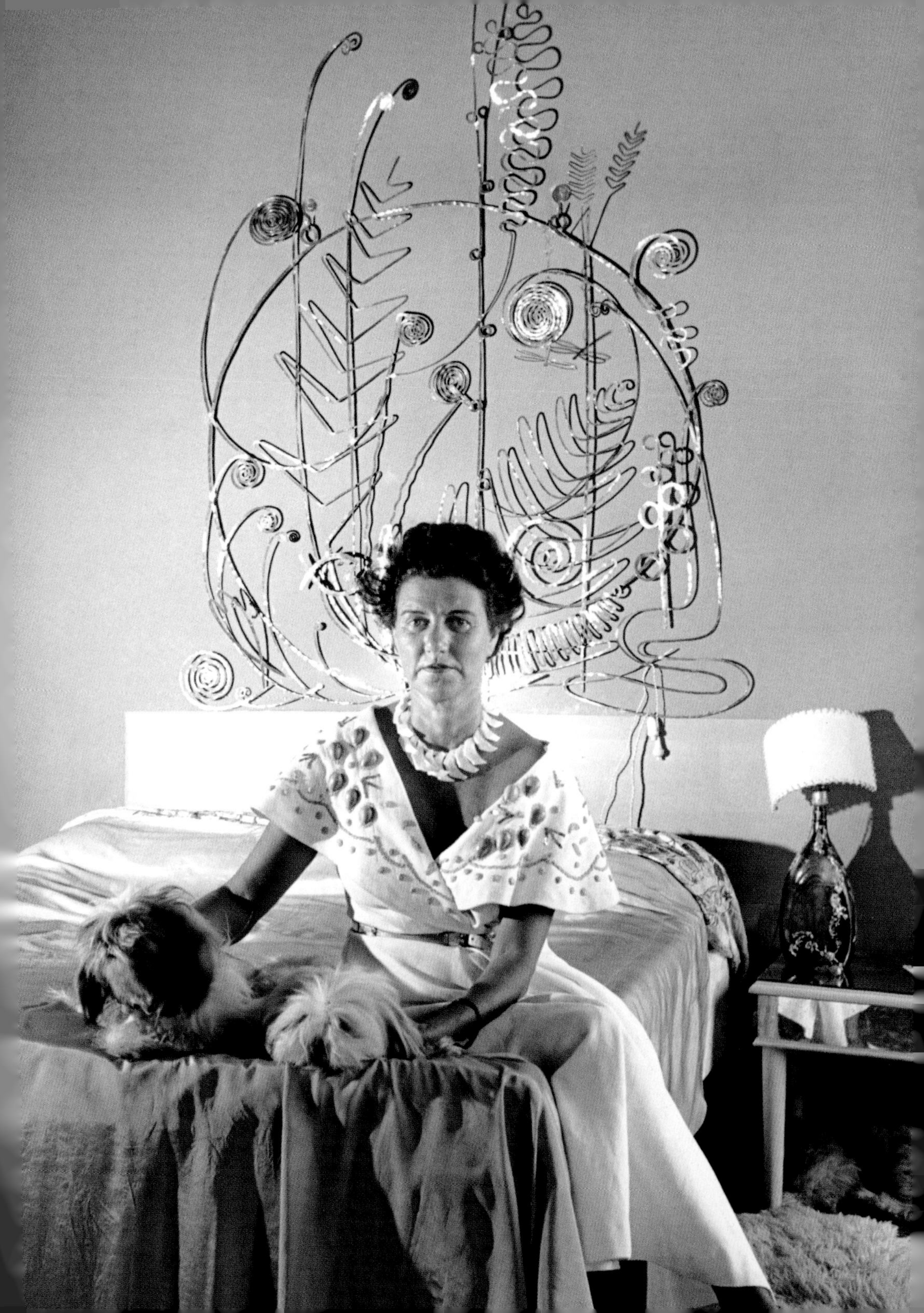

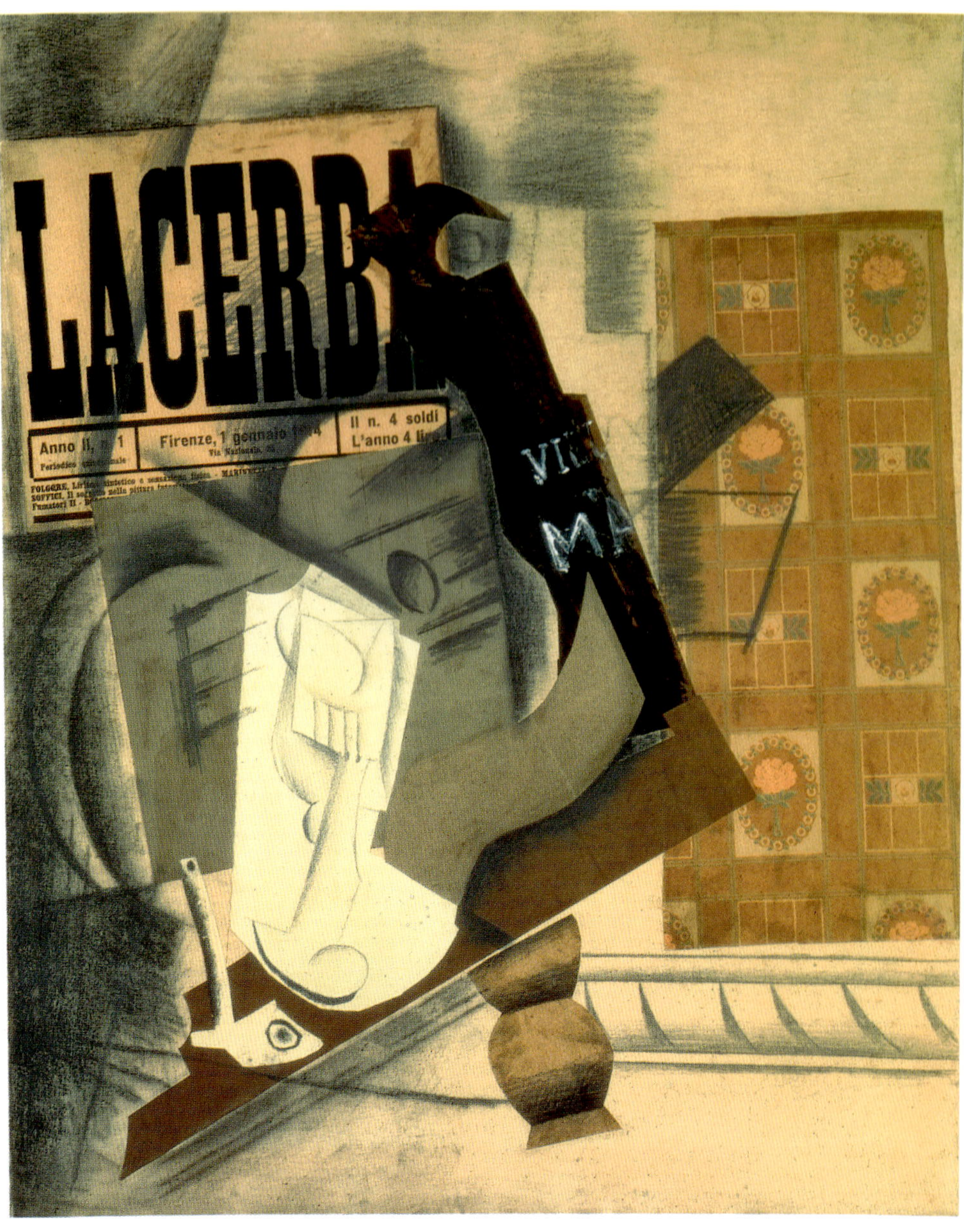

LACERBA
Anno II, N. 1
Periodico quindicinale
Firenze, 1 gennaio 1914
Via Nazionale, 26
Il n. 4 soldi
L'anno 4 lire
VIE
MA

Chronology

1898: Peggy Guggenheim is born in New York City on West 69th Street, the daughter of Benjamin Guggenheim and Florette Seligman.

1912: Benjamin Guggenheim dies in the *Titanic* disaster, leaving the family in an awful financial situation after he lost almost all his fortune in Paris.

1919: In the summer, Peggy begins to receive money from her trust fund. The first thing she does is to make an extensive trip all over the United States, from Niagara Falls to the border of Mexico.

1920: In the winter, she decides to have an operation to change the shape of her nose. But everything goes wrong. If her nose was ugly before, it is undoubtedly worse afterwards.

1921: In Paris, at the age of 23, she dreams of losing her virginity and making love in various positions (which she saw in a book about Pompeii frescos). She decides to try it with her fiancé, Laurence Vail, the self-proclaimed "King of Bohemia." He will become her husband and the father of her two children: Pegeen and Sindbad.

1927: Peggy suffers terribly when her favorite sister, Benita, dies in childbirth.

1928: In St Tropez, she meets John Holms, an alcoholic writer. It is love at first sight, and they leave their respective families to live together. Peggy always referred to Holms as the great love of her life. In 1934, Holms dies of a heart attack after an operation.

1937: Peggy falls madly in love with Samuel Beckett, but the relationship does not last. Her mother dies and Peggy decides to open an art gallery, hoping to overcome her sorrow.

1938: Opening of her first avant-garde gallery in London, Guggenheim Jeune. With Marcel Duchamp as her adviser, she produces important exhibitions for Cocteau and Kandinsky.

1939: In Paris, Peggy buys one masterpiece a day.

1941: On July 13, Peggy, her collection, and a group of eleven other people (including her future husband, Max Ernst) fly to New York.

1942: After seemingly endless complications, Peggy marries Max Ernst in Virginia.
On October 20, Peggy opens the gallery Art of This Century in New York, a sensational space created for her by the avant-garde architect Friedrich Kiesler.

1946: In March, Peggy's memoirs, *Out of This Century*, is published by Dial Press with a cover designed by Jackson Pollock. The scandalized Guggenheims, calling the book *Out of Her Mind*, send a horde of messengers to buy up every available copy.

1947: Peggy decides to close Art of This century. Back in Europe, she accompanies Mary McCarthy and her husband to Venice.

Pipe, Glass, Bottle of Vieux Marc by Pablo Picasso, 1914. Paper collage, charcoal, india ink, printer's ink, graphite, and gouache on canvas, 19^{1/3} x 23^{2/3}". © 2003 Estate of Pablo Picasso/ADAGP, Paris.

1948: Peggy is invited to show her entire collection at the XXIV Biennale in Venice. The exhibition gets enormous publicity and becomes one of the most popular events.

1949: Peggy buys an unfinished palace on the Grand Canal; it was previously owned by the Veniers, a famous Venetian family.

1950: Peggy is proud to personally organize a retrospective of Jackson Pollock's paintings for the Museo Correr in Saint Mark Square, in Venice.

1952: Peggy sponsors a young Italian painter, Tancredi.

1954: Raoul Gregorich, Peggy's last lover, dies in a car crash. Desperate, she flies to Ceylon to visit her friend Paul Bowles on his island.

1956: After Jackson Pollock's death in a car crash near East Hampton on August 11, Peggy and Jackson's wife, Lee Krasner, feud over the ownership of a number of paintings.

1959: Peggy invites me to accompany her on a journey to Greece.

1960: Peggy writes a wonderful introduction to a book called *Invitation to Venice*, with photographs by Ugo Mulas and text by Michelangelo Muraro.

1961: Peggy asks Claire Falkenstein to create new gates for the entrance of her palace. The result is stunning. In the street, everyone stops to admire the "Gates of Heaven," as Peggy calls them.

1962: Peggy is made an honorary citizen of Venice. The ceremony takes place in the town hall.

1965: Peggy is invited to show her collection in London (the Tate Gallery hopes to inherit it) and I accompany her. The show is a terrific success, with people queuing up along the Embarkment.

1966: A most terrible flood occurs in Venice. Peggy becomes an honorary member of "Save Venice" and gives a large amount of money to John Mac Andrew, its former chairman.

1967: Peggy is made a *commendatore* of the Italian Republic, and is given a parchment and a medal. Because of her daughter's death, she refuses to attend the ceremony.

1969: Exhibition of Peggy's collection in the Guggenheim Museum in New York. She reaches an agreement with cousin her cousin Harry regarding the future of the collection.

1975: She is invited to show her collection at the Orangerie, in Paris. This is a great honor as well as a revenge—the Louvre had refused to save the collection in 1940.

1978: To celebrate Peggy eightieth birthday, Dr. Passante, the director of the Gritti Hotel, gives a dinner party for her and her friends. There is a banner with her name on it: TO THE ULTIMA DOGARESSA.

1979: Peggy dies. The Palazzo Venier dei Leoni and the beloved collection become the property of the Solomon R. Foundation in New York.

The Surrealist *by Victor Brauner, 1947, oil on canvas, 24 x 18". The table is also an insect, a flying fish, or a sort of dog.*
Reality is magically transformed. © Akg-images/ADAGP.

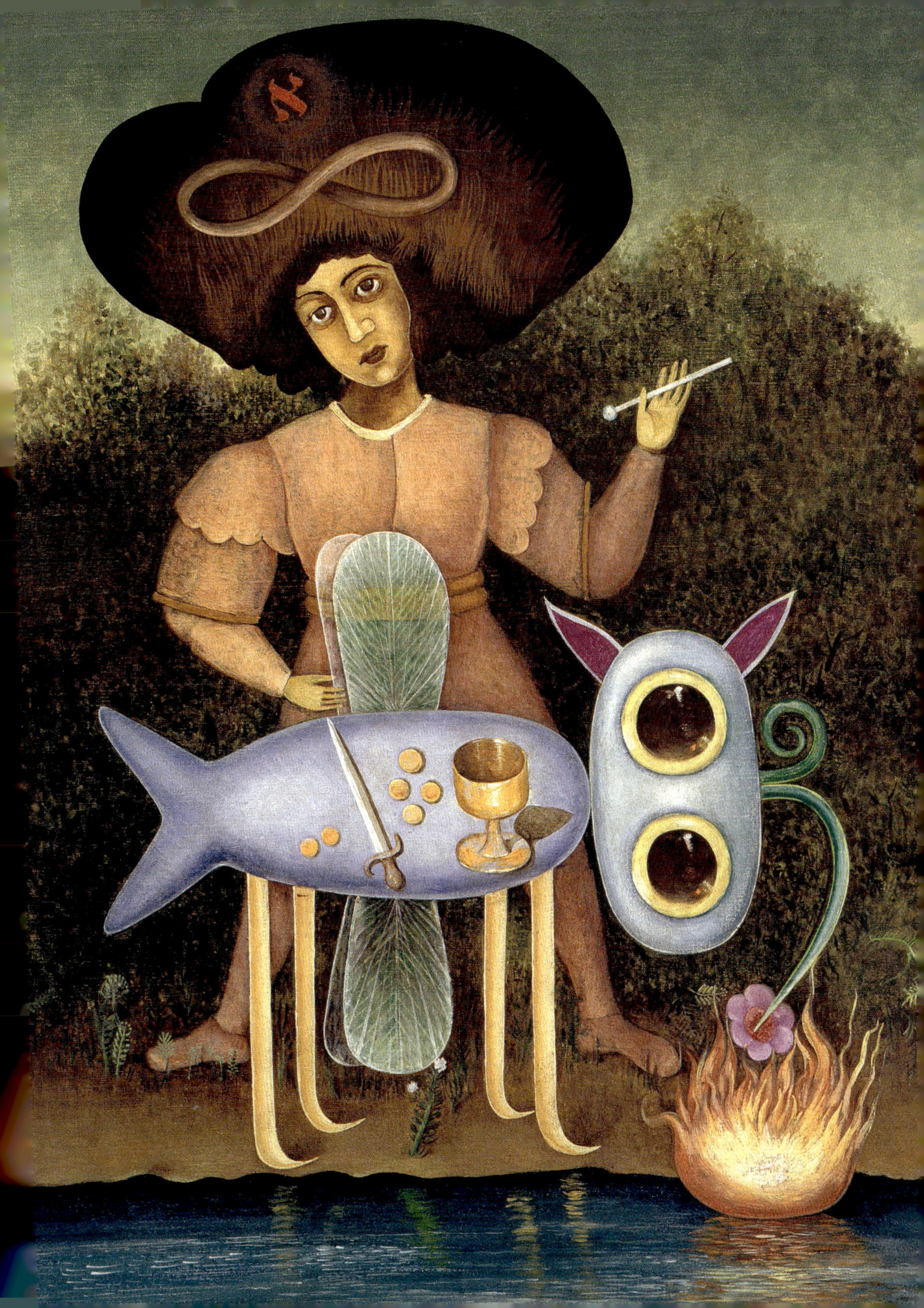

The Collection established by Peggy Guggenheim

Alechinsky, Pierre, *Dressing Gown*, 1972

Apollonio, Marina, *Relief No. 505*, 1968

Appel, Karel, *The Crocodile*, 1956

Archipenko, Alexander, *Boxers*, 1935

Arman, *Variable & Invariable*, 1963

Armitage, Kenneth, *Diarchy*, 1957

Armitage, Kenneth,
People in the Wind, 1951

Arp, Jean, *Amphora Fruit*, 1951

Arp, Jean, *Composition*, 1915

Arp, Jean, *Drawing*, 1940

Arp, Jean, *Garland of Buds I*, 1936

Arp, Jean, *Maimed and Stateless*, 1936

Arp, Jean, *Overturned Blue Shoe
with Tow Heels under a Black Vault*, 1925

Arp, Jean, *Shell and Head*, 1933

Bacci, Edmondo, *Event 286*, 1958

Bacci, Edmondo, *Event 292*, 1958

Bacon, Francis,
Study for Chimpanzee, 1957

Baj, Enrico, *Get Lost*, 1967

Balla, Giacomo,
Automobile and Noise, 1912

Baziotes, William, *Gouache*, 1943

Baziotes, William, *The Room*, 1945

Boccioni, Umberto, *Dynamic Construction
of a Gallop - Horse - House*, 1913

Boto, Martha, *Structure Optique*, 1963

Brancusi, Constantin, *Bird in Space*, 1940

Brancusi, Constantin, *Maiastra*, 1915

Braque, Georges,
Still Life [The Waltz], 1912

Braque, Georges, *Still Life*, 1926

Brauner, Victor,
Consciousness of Shock, 1951

Brauner, Victor, *Painting on wax*, 1945

Brauner, Victor, *Painting on wax*, 1954

Brauner, Victor, *Téléventré*, 1948

Brauner, Victor, *The Surrealist*, 1947

Brauner, Victor,
Three gouaches in one, 1941

Brô, René, *Autumn at Courgeron*, 1960

Butler, Reg, *Woman Walking*, 1951

Calder, Alexander, *Glass Mobile*, 1950

Calder, Alexander,
Le Grand Passage, 1974

Calder, Alexander, *Mobile*, 1941

Calder, Alexander, *Silver Bed Head*, 1945

Campigli, Massimo, *Ball Game*, 1960

Carrington, Leonora, *Oink (They Shall
Behold Thine Eyes)*, 1959

César (Baldaccini, César),
Compression, 1969

César (Baldaccini, César),
Man in a Spider's Web, 1955

Chadwick, Lynn,
Maquette for Teddy Boy and Girl, 1955

Chagall, Marc, *Rain*, 1911

Congdon, William, *Cambodia*, 1960

Congdon, William,
Piazza San Marco, 1957

Congdon, William, *Venice*, 1957

Consagra, Pietro,
Mythical Conference, 1959

Corneille (Beverloo, Corneille Guillaume),
Great Solar Symphony, 1964

Cornell, Joseph, *Hôtel de l'Ange*, 1940s

Cornell, Joseph,
Parrot Music Box, 1937-38

Cornell, Joseph, *Pharmacy*, 1943

Cornell, Joseph,
Setting for a Fairy Tale, 1942-46

Cornell, Joseph, *Soap Bubble Box*, 1941

Costa, Toni, *Visual Dynamic*, 1964

Costalonga, Franco,
Sphere of plexiglass, 1969
Dalì, Salvador,
The Birth of Liquid Desires, 1932
Dalì, Salvador,
Woman Sleeping in a Landscape, 1931
Davie, Alan, *Orange Jumper*, 1960
Davie, Alan,
The Golden Drummer Boy No. 2, 1962
Davie, Alan, *Untitled*, 1950
De Chirico, Giorgio,
The Dream of the Poet, 1914
De Chirico, Giorgio,
The Gentle Afternoon, 1916
De Chirico, Giorgio, *The Rose Tower*, 1913
De Kooning, Willem, *Composition*, 1958
De Kooning, Willem, *Drawing*, 1958
De Luigi, Ludovico, *Parnassus Apollo
and Papilio Macaon*, 1970
Delaunay, Robert, *Windows*, 1912
Delvaux, Paul, *The Break of a Day*, 1937
Dorazio, Piero, *Unitas*, 1965
Dubuffet, Jean,
Châtaine aux Hautes Chairs, 1951
Duchamp, Marcel,
Sad Young Man in a Train, 1911
Duchamp, Marcel,
The Duchamp Valise, 1941-42
Duchamp-Villon, Raymond,
The Horse, 1914
Dzamonja, Duan, *Totem*, 1959
Ernst, Max,
Garden Airplane Trap, 1935-36
Ernst, Max, *In the Streets of Athens*, 1960
Ernst, Max, *Little Machine Constructed
by Minimax Dadamax in Person*, 1919
Ernst, Max, *Sea. Sun. Earthquake*, 1931
Ernst, Max, *The Anti-Pope*, 1941
Ernst, Max,
The Attirement of the Bride, 1940
Ernst, Max, *The Entire City*, 1937
Ernst, Max, *The Forest*, 1928
Ernst, Max, *The Kiss*, 1927

Ernst, Max, *The Postman Cheval*, 1932
Ernst, Max, *Woman Flower*, 1944
Ernst, Max, *Zoomorphic Couple*, 1933
Falkenstein,
Claire, Entrance Gates to Palace, 1961
Ferren, John, *Tempora*, 1937
Fini, Leonor,
The Shepherdess of the Sphinxes, 1941
Francis, Sam, *Tobago*, 1964
Giacometti, Alberto,
Lion Woman, 1946-47
Giacometti, Alberto,
Model for a Garden, 1932
Giacometti, Alberto, *Piazza*, 1948-49
Giacometti, Alberto, *Statue of a Headless
Woman*, 1932-36 (bronze)
Giacometti, Alberto, *Statue of a Headless
Woman*, 1932-36 (plaster)
Giacometti, Alberto,
Woman with a Cut Throat, 1932-33
Gilardi, Rosalba, *Presence*, 1967
Gleizes, Albert,
Woman with Animals, 1914
Gonzales, Julio, *Cactus Man I*, 1939-40
Gorky, Arshile, *Painting*, 1944
Gris, Juan,
The Bottle of Martinique Rum, 1914
Guzmán, Alberto,
Partizione percotente, 1965
Hare, David, *Moon Cage*, 1955
Hartigan, Grace, *Ireland*, 1958
Hausmann, Raoul, *Watercolour*, 1919
Hayter, S. W., *Defeat*, 1938-39
Hélion, Jean, *Equilibrium*, 1933-34
Hélion, Jean, *Large Volumes*, 1935
Hirshfield, Morris,
Two Mowen in Front of a Mirror, 1943
Hundertwasser, Fritz,
Protecting House, 1960
Irwin, Gwyther, *Serendipity 2*, 1957
Jorn, Asger, *Figures*, 1957
Kandinsky, Wassily, *Landscape
with Church II (with red pot)*, 1913

Kandinsky, Wassily, *Upward*, 1929
Kandinsky, Wassily, *White Cross*, 1922
Kemeny, Zoltan, *Divided Movement*, 1957
Klee, Paul, *Magic Garden*, 1926
Klee, Paul,
Portrait of Mme P. in the South, 1924
Koczy, Rosemarie Heber, *Trees*, 1972
Koenig, Fritz, *The Chariot*, 1957
Kupka, Frantisek,
Around a Point, c. 1914
Kupka, Frantisek, *Dynamic*, 1912
Kupka, Frantisek,
Étude Chromatique, 1910
Kupka, Frantisek,
Study for a Fugue, 1911
Kupka, Frantisek, *Vertical Plans*, 1911-12
Lardera, Berto,
Dramatic Meeting III, 1956
Lassaw, Ibram, *Corax*, 1953
Laurens, Henri, *Head of a Girl*, 1920
Léger, Fernand, *Contraste de formes*, (no date)
Léger, Fernand, *Men in the City*, 1919
Léger, Fernand,
Nude Model in the Studio, 1912-13
Leonid, *Venetian Lagoon*, (no date)
Lipchitz, Jacques, *Aurelia*, 1964
Lipchitz, Jacques, *Seated Pierrot*, 1921
Lissitzky, El, *Composition*, 1921
Mack, Heinz,
Cardiogram of an Angel, 1964
Magritte, René,
Domain of Lights, 1953-54
Magritte, René, *Voice of the Winds*, 1932
Malevitch, Kasimir,
Suprematist Composition, 1915
Marcoussis, Louis, *The Habitué*, 1920
Marini, Marino,
The Angel of the Citadel, 1949
Massironi, Manfredo,
Ipercubo Plexiglass, 1962
Masson, André,
Bird Fascinated by a Snake, 1943
Masson, André, *L'Armure*, 1925

Masson, André, *Two Children*, 1942
Matta, Drawing, 1941
Matta,
The Un-Nominator Renominated, 1953
Metzinger, Jean,
The Cycle-Racing Track, 1914
Minguzzi, Luciano, *He-Goat*, 1956
Mirko (Basaldella, Mirko),
Architectural Element, 1953
Mirko (Basaldella, Mirko),
Little Chimera, 1956
Miró, Joan, *Dutch Interior II*, 1928
Miró, Joan, *Seated Woman II*, 1939
Miró, Joan,
Two Personages and a Flame, 1925
Mondrian, Piet,
Composition with Red, 1939
Mondrian, Piet, *Scaffolding*, 1912
Mondrian, Piet, *The Sea*, 1914
Moore, Henry, *Drawing*, 1937
Moore, Henry, *Family Group*, 1946
Moore, Henry, *Ideas for Sculpture*, 1937
Moore, Henry, *Reclining Figure*, 1938
Moore, Henry, *String Figure*, 1938
Moore, Henry,
Three Standing Figures, 1946
Motherwell, Robert,
Surprise and Inspiration, 1943
Nele, E. R., *Collective II*, 1961
Nicholson, Ben, February 1956 (menhir)
Oelze, Richard, *Drawing*, c. 1933
Okada, Kenzo, *Above the White*, 1960
Ozenfant, Amédée,
Guitar and Bottles, 1920
Paolozzi, Eduardo, *Chinese Dog 2*, 1958
Pevsner, Antoine,
Cross in the Form of an Anchor, 1934
Pevsner, Antoine,
Developable Surface, 1938
Pevsner, Antoine,
Developable Surface, 1941
Picabia, Francis,
Very Rare Picture upon the Earth, 1915

Picasso, Pablo,
Bust of a Man in a Striped Jersey, 1939
Picasso, Pablo, *Girls with a Toy Boat*
[On the Beach], 1937
Picasso, Pablo, *Lacerba [Pipe, Verre,*
Bouteille de Vieux Marc], 1914
Picasso, Pablo,
The Dream and Lie of Franco, 1937
Picasso, Pablo, *The Poet*, 1911
Picasso, Pablo, *The Studio*, 1928
Pollock, Jackson, *Alchemy*, 1947
Pollock, Jackson, *Bird Effort*, 1946
Pollock, Jackson, *Circumcision*, 1946
Pollock, Jackson, *Direction*, 1945
Pollock, Jackson, *Don Quixote*, 1944
Pollock, Jackson, *Enchanted Forest*, 1947
Pollock, Jackson, *Eyes in the Heat*, 1946
Pollock, Jackson, *Gouache*, 1946
Pollock, Jackson, *Moon Woman*, 1942
Pollock, Jackson,
Sounds in the Grass, 1946
Pollock, Jackson, *Two*, 1945
Pomodoro, Arnaldo, *Relief*, 1961
Pomodoro, Arnaldo, *Sphere No. 1*, 1963
Ray, Emanuel (known as Man),
Silhouette, 1916
Ray, Emanuel (known as Man),
Two Rayographs, 1923 and 1927
Richier, Germaine, *Tauromachy*, 1953
Richter, Hans, *Dada Kopf*, 1918
Richter, Hans, *Dada Kopf*, 1923
Riopelle, Jean-Paul, *Painting*, 1955
Rothko, Mark, *Sacrifice*, 1943
Santomaso, Giuseppe, *Hidden Life*, 1958
Schwitters, Kurt, *Blue on Blue*, 1929
Schwitters, Kurt, *Merzbild*, 1930
Schwitters, Kurt, *Mz 75*, 1920
Severini, Gino, *Dancer = Sea*, 1913
Sobrino, Francisco, *Transformation*
Instable Superposition-Juxtaposition, 1963
Still, Clyfford, *Jamais*, 1944
Sutherland, Graham,
Organic Form, 1962-68

Takis, *Signal*, 1958
Tamayo, Rufino, *Heavenly Bodies*, 1946
Tancredi, *Composition*, 1956
Tancredi, serie of gouaches
Tanguy, Yves, *Gouache*, 1938
Tanguy, Yves, *On Slanting Ground*, 1941
Tanguy, Yves, *Portrait of P. G.*, 1938
Tanguy, Yves,
Promontory Palace, 1930 or 1931
Tanguy, Yves, *The Sun in its Casket*, 1937
Thornton, Leslie, *Roundabout*, 1955
Tobey, Marc, *Advance of History*, 1964
Toyofuky, Tomonori,
"Drifting" No. 2, 1959
Tunnard, John, *PSI*, 1938
Tunnard, John, *Watercolour*, 1941
Uecker, Gunther, *Nail Construction*, 1962
Vail, Laurence, *Screen*, 1940
Vail, Laurence, *Series of decorated bottles*
and assembled objects, 1940-55
Vail, Pegeen, *In the Park*, 1953
Vail, Pegeen, *My Wedding*, 1946
Vail, Pegeen,
series of oils and pastels, 1954-55
Van Doesburg, Theo, *Composition*, 1918
Van Doesburg, Theo,
Counter-Composition, 1926
Vantongerloo, Georges, *Construction*
in an Inscribed and a Circumscribed
Square of a Circle, 1924
Vasarely, Victor, *Yak*, 1964
Vedova, Emilio, *Hostage City*, 1954
Vedova, Emilio,
Image of our Time (Barricade), 1951
Villon, Jacques, *Spaces*, 1920

All the works can be admired at
the Peggy Guggenheim museum:
Palazzo Venier dei Leoni
701 Dorsoduro
30123 Venice

Peggy Guggenheim Collection

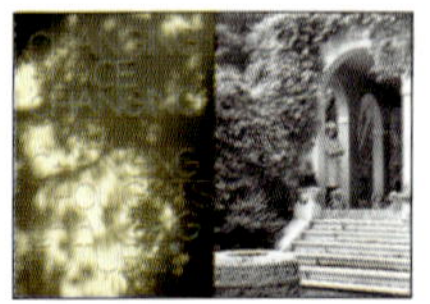

Maurizio Nannucci's 2003 neon work *Changing Place, Changing Time, Changing Thoughts, Changing Future*. Commissioned for the museum's recent survey on 20th century sculpture at the Foro Boario, it has been re-installed in the garden beside the Museum Café. © Assouline.
Peggy outside the *Barchessa*, the elegant portico that can be found in most Venetian palaces and villas. Peggy decided to build a wing in her garden when there was no more space in the house for the paintings of her collection. She copied as closely as possible the Palladian architecture of the wing built for the villa Emo at Fanzolo. © Courtesy P. Barozzi, Aschieri Torino.

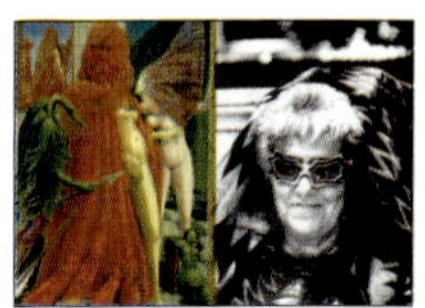

The Attirement of the Bride by Max Ernst, 1940, oil on canvas, 51" x 38½". © Akg-images Cameraphoto/ADAGP.
A close-up of Peggy by Roloff Beny, taken in the late 1960s. Peggy is wearing a black and gold sari, a present from the Maharani of Berar, and sunglasses created by Yves Tanguy. Peggy had a collection of sunglasses and enjoyed wearing them in front of the camera. Some were created for her by such artists as Yves Tanguy and Edward Melcarth. © Roloff Benny.

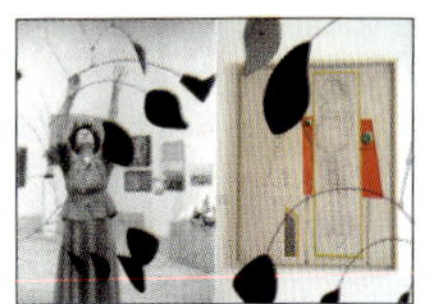

Peggy arranging her Calder mobile in the Greek Pavillion before the opening of the XXIV Venice Biennale, in 1948. © Roloff Beny. *The Studio* by Pablo Picasso, 1928, oil on canvas, 63⅝ x 51⅛". By 1928, Picasso had moved away from cubism and toward surrealism, but some traces of the synthetic cubist style are still present in the flat, overlapping planes of this work. The figures are depicted in a completely arbitrary linear style. The figure on the left can also be read as piece of sculpture set on a plinth, and that on the right as a painting on canvas; the effect is deliberately imprecise and ambiguous. © Assouline.

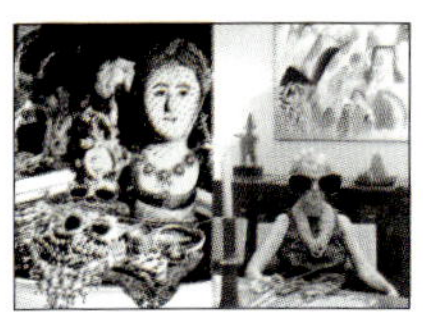

Peggy's eccentric jewels. She enjoyed wearing them, and thought they underlined the enigmatic side of her personality. She owned a great number of necklaces and earrings, some she created herself, and others were created by famous artists; they were found in Venice or during her travels around the world. © Roloff Beny. **Peggy sitting in her dining room** (1960), with behind her, a painting by Kandinsky. She is wearing a pair of enormous sunglasses, and looks like the queen bee, one of her surrealist interpretations. On the table are three sunglasses (designed by Edward Melcarth), which she used as masks for her surrealist disguises. © Akg-images/Bianconero.

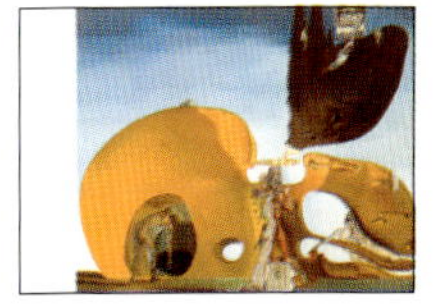

The Birth of Liquid Desires by Salvador Dalì, 1932, oil on canvas, 38½ x 44⅞". Toward the end of the 1930s, Peggy had bought two small paintings by Dalì, yet she wanted a masterpiece for her collection. During the war she went to Dalì's apartment in Paris and bought this major work from Gala, the painter's wife. © Dagli Orti/ADAGP.

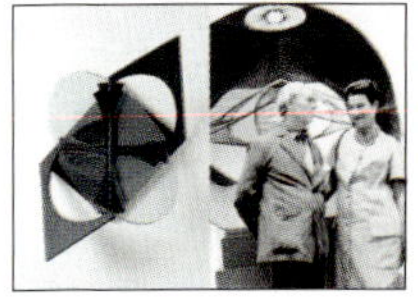

Anchored Cross by Antoine Pevsner, 1934, marble, brass painted black, and crystal. Pevsner was the elder brother of the sculptor Naum Gabo. Together they set forth the principles of constructivism in the *Realist Manifesto*. © Artists Rights Society (ARS), New York/ADAGP, Paris.
Peggy with Antoine Pevsner, in front of one of his constructions. Pevsner was a timid little man who reminded Peggy of Al Jolson's joke: "Are you man or mouse?" Pevsner conceived a great passion for Peggy, but thinking he was more a mouse than a man, she did not reciprocate his feeling. They were nonetheless great friends. © Courtesy Paolo Barozzi.

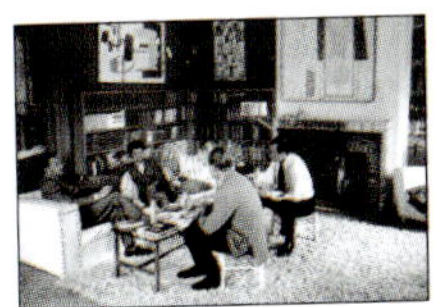

Peggy with friends in her palace. She loved entertaining famous writers: here she is with Tennessee Williams (seated on her right). Back to the camera is fashion designer Ken Scott, one of Peggy's dearest friends. © All Rights Reserved.

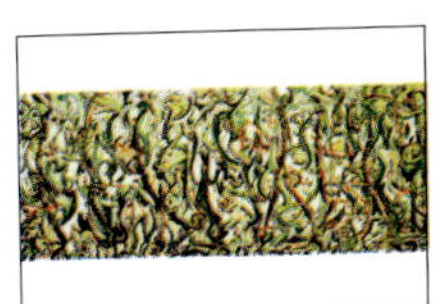

Mural by Jackson Pollock, 1943, oil on canvas, 99 x 242″. A gift from Peggy Guggenheim to the University of Iowa Museum of Art. © Akg-images/ADAGP.

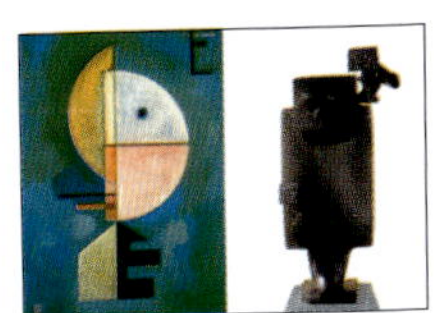

Upwards by Wassily Kandinsky, 1929, oil on cardboard, 28 x 19$^{1/2}$″. © Akg-images/ADAGP.

In the Street of Athens by Max Ernst, 1960, bronze, 39$^{1/3}$ x 19$^{4/5}$ x 7$^{1/3}$″. This sculpture was made in Ernst's studio in Touraine. © Assouline/ADAGP.

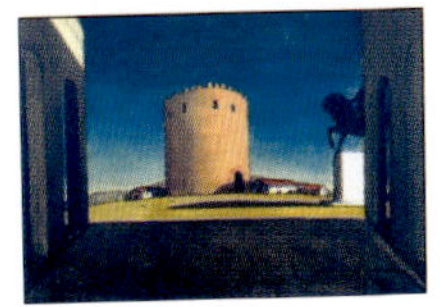

The Red Tower by Giorgio De Chirico, 1913, oil on canvas, 29$^{1/3}$ x 40″. After living in Turin, Milan, and Florence, De Chirico moved to Paris in July 1911, and began to paint a series of strange, dreamlike townscapes evocative of Italian piazzas. He described this picture as "a piazza with arcades on the sides. In the background, behind a wall, appears an equestrian monument similar to those dedicated to soldiers and heroes of the Risorgimento, which one can see in so many Italian cities, and particularly in Turin. © Akg-images/ADAGP.

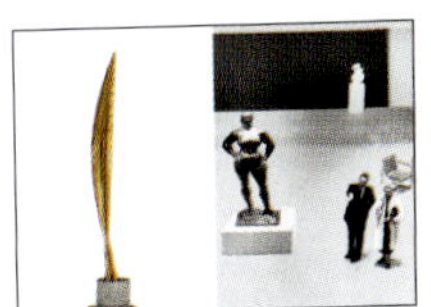

Bird in Space by Constantin Brancusi, 1940, polished brass, 60$^{2/3}$″ (height). This golden perfection is the most precious jewel of the collection. Peggy had wanted to buy a Brancusi bronze for years, and in particular *Bird in Space*, but Brancusi did not want to sell that particular work. He finally accepted Peggy's offer. When Peggy went to fetch the sculpture, tears were streaming down Brancusi's face. © 2003 ADAGP Paris.

Peggy visiting the Brooklyn Museum in New York with its curator, in 1959. She was back in New York after twelve years abroad. © Roloff Benny.

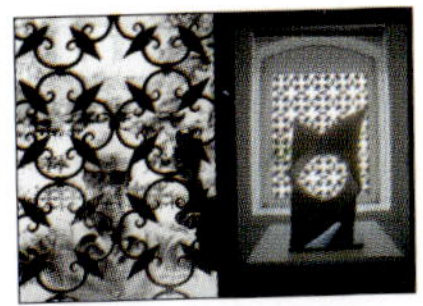

A photo which can be considered emblematic. Who is the mysterious lady hiding behind the big surreal sunglasses, and the wrought iron gates? A muse of the arts, a woman whose eccentric public image hid her feelings, her shyness, and her fears. An incurable romantic looking toward life and the world. © Courtesy Paolo Barozzi, All Rights Reserved.

Developable Surface by Antoine Pevsner, 1938, bronze and copper, 20$^{4/5}$ x 12$^{1/4}$″. © Assouline.

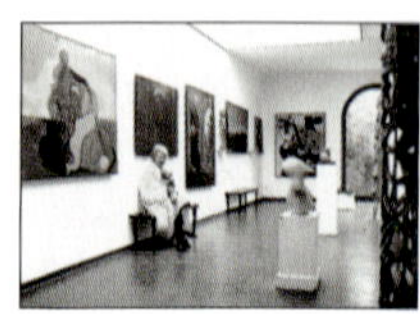

Peggy seated in the *Barchessa*. Behind her, the paintings are by Max Ernst (from left to right): *The Kiss* (1927), *The Forest* (1928), *Attirement of the Bride* (1940). On the wall near the window is *Seated Woman II* (1939) by Joan Miró, and in front of Peggy, the sculpture is *Crown of Buds I* (1936), by Jean Arp. © Roloff Benny.

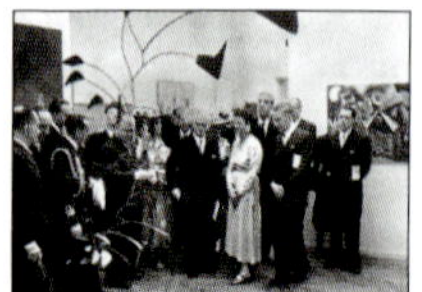

Peggy with Luigi Einaudi, the president of Italy, in 1948; Peggy was invited to show her collection at the XXIV Venice Biennale. The exhibition was a great success, but what Peggy enjoyed most was seeing the name Guggenheim next to those of the big nations of the world.
Courtesy Paolo Barozzi. © All Rights Reserved.

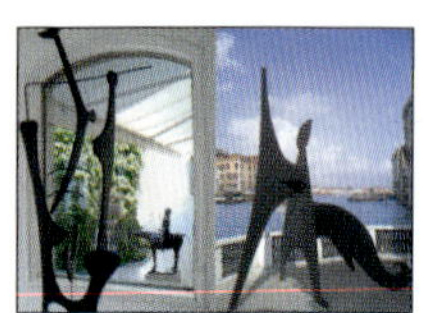

In the distance, ***The Angel of the Citadel*** by Marino Marini. It is a statue of a rider, with his arms spread out in ecstasy. When Marino cast the sculpture with bronze, he had the phallus made separately, so that it could be removed at leisure. In Venice, a legend spread that Peggy had several phalluses of different sizes, like spare parts, which she used on different occasions. © Assouline.
One of Calder's stabile. It did not belong to Peggy's collection, but was bought by the museum after her death. © Assouline.

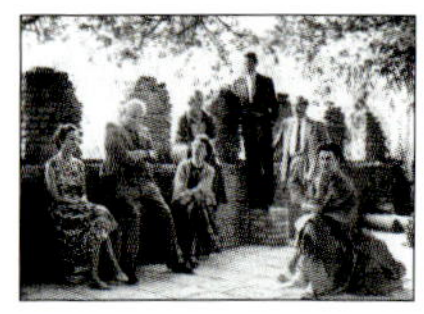

Peggy and friends photographed by Roloff Beny, in 1958, at the villa Condulmer near Venice. From left to right: the writer Nancy Mitford, Lord Cunard, the Countess Marina Cicogna Volpi, the baroness Alix de Rothschild, Philip van Renseler, and Arthur Jeffries. © Roloff Beny.

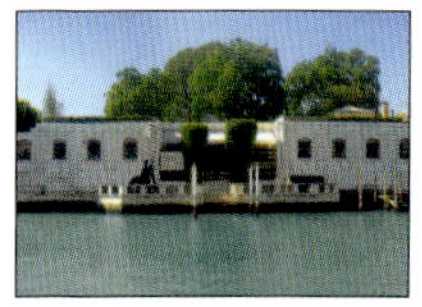

After showing her collection at the XXIV Venice Biennale, in 1949, Peggy buys an unfinished palace, **the Palazzo Venier dei Leoni.** It has the widest access to the Grand Canal, and at the back, one of the largest gardens in Venice. In this house lived the legendary Marchesa Luisa Casati. © Assouline.

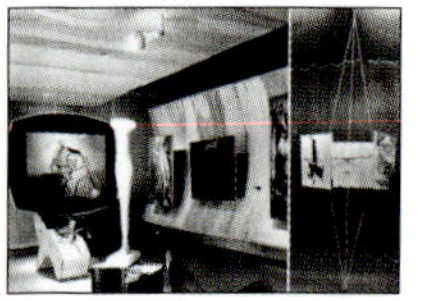

The Surrealist Gallery at Art of This Century, in New York. The curved walls are made of gum wood, and the unframed paintings were mounted on baseball bats. Each picture had its own spotlight, which went on and off every three seconds—to everybody's dismay. © All Rights Reserved.
The Abstract and Cubist Gallery at Art of This Century. The paintings were clustered in triangles and hung on strings, thus floating in space. In front, a sculpture by Alberto Giacometti. © All Rights Reserved.

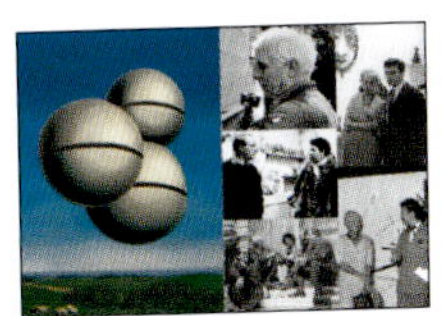

Voice of Space by René Magritte, 1932, oil on canvas, 30¹ᐟ³ x 21²ᐟ³". © Akg-images/ADAGP.
From top to bottom, left to right: **Max Ernst**; **Peggy Guggenheim and Paolo Barozzi** in Venice, in 1960; **Henry Moore and Peggy Guggenheim**; **Peggy Guggenheim** in 1967, the day she was made *commendatore* of the Italian Republic; **Peggy and Mathieu**. © Courtesy Paolo Barozzi, Roloff Benny, All Rights Reserved.

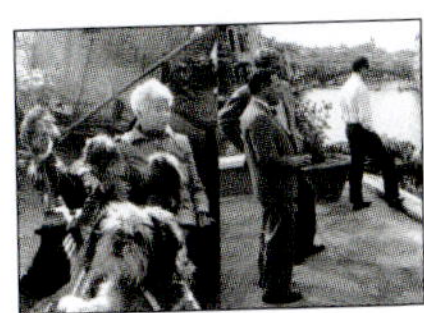

Peggy in her gondola, which she had made to order. The gondola was beautifully carved with lions, and to go out in it at sunset, with her dogs, was one of Peggy's greatest pleasures. © Courtesy Paolo Barozzi, All Rights Reserved.
Tennessee Williams and Ken Scott looking at the Grand Canal from Peggy's roof terrace. © Courtesy Paolo Barozzi, Lifephoto by Frank Scherschel.

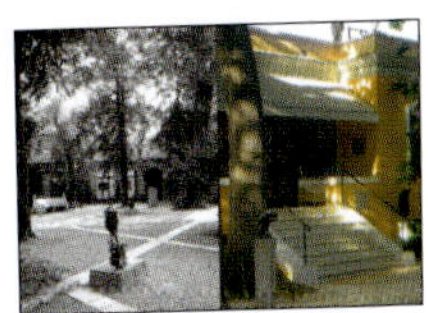

The garden of the Palazzo Venier dei Leoni, and in the center, *Tauromachy* by Germaine Richier. © Courtesy Paolo Barozzi, All Rights Reserved.
The entrance to the collection; the large staircase was used as a stage for the masques written to celebrate Peggy's birthday. © Assouline.

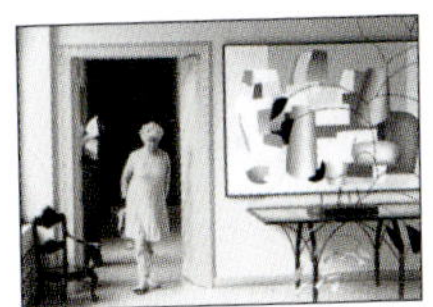

Peggy Guggenheim in her palazzo; behind her is *Developable Surface* by Antoine Pevsner; next to her are: on the wall, *Composition* by Jean Helion, 1935, on the table, *Piazza* by Alberto Giacometti, 1948, and in the foreground, a mobile by Alexander Calder, 1941. © Courtesy Paolo Barozzi, All Rights Reserved.

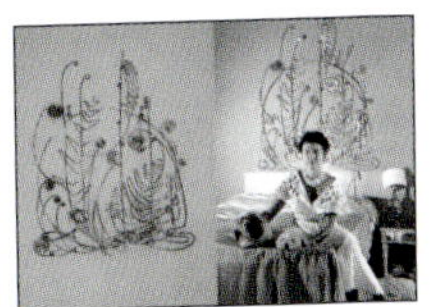

Bedhead by Alexander Calder. In 1946, Peggy asked Calder to make a bedhead for her. Because of the war, the only material available was silver, and the result was, therefore, not a mobile (except for the fish and butterfly that swung in the background). Peggy was the only woman in the world to sleep in a Calder bed. © Assouline.
Peggy with two of her Lhasa Apso, in 1950. © David Seymour/Gamma.

The author would like to thank Kay Guttmann for the work she has done.
He also wishes to thank Mr. and Mrs. Philip Rylands of the Peggy Guggenheim
Collection in Venice, Attilio Codognato, Roloff Benny, and Ken Scott.